Also by Brigitte van Tuijl

*The Gap – bridge the space between where
you are and where you want to be*

The Art of Divine Selfishness Series

*Book One: Unmute Your Life – break free from
fear & go for what you REALLY want*

*Book Two: The Art of Divine Selfishness – transform your
life, your business & the world by putting YOU first*

Books in Dutch

Ontdek Wat Je Écht Wilt En Maak Daar (Je) Werk Van

THE INNER MINIMALIST

CLEAR THE CLUTTER OF YOUR MIND
FOR A SIMPLER, QUIETER AND HAPPIER LIFE

BRIGITTE VAN TUIJL

ISBN Paperback: 978-90-830654-6-5
ISBN e-book: 978-90-830654-7-2

Visit www.booksbybrigitte.com for more books by the author.
For additional gifts, visit www.innerminimalistgifts.com

The information provided in this book is designed to inspire, educate,
motivate, and enlighten you on the subjects discussed. It's not meant as a
substitute for professional coaching or other expert assistance. If such level
of assistance is required, please seek the services of a competent professional
or contact the author directly for one-to-one coaching options. The author
assumes no liability for use of the information and exercises.

Copy editor: Kelly Urgan
Cover design: Susan D. Johnson
Interior Design: FormattedBooks.com

CONTENTS

Part 3 — The Truth About You

Part 4 — How to Live from Your Soul

INTRODUCTION

So many people are stressed out, burned out, overworked, overwhelmed, unhappy and unfulfilled. We constantly look for meaning and calm in a loud and busy world.

Everyone looks for it in different ways. Some try consuming less, or living off grid, or moving into a tiny house or living mortgage free. Others hop from one life coach to the next or read one self-help book after another. Some don't know where to start and instead numb or distract themselves with alcohol, drugs, watching TV or doing anything else that takes their mind off of what they're missing in their lives.

What most of these ways have in common is that they focus on something *outside* of yourself. Yes, changing your *outer* life can impact how you feel on the inside. Living mortgage free can enhance your sense of freedom—until your money disappears and you feel trapped again. Clearing out your attic can give you a sense of spaciousness—until a couple of months later, when new clutter takes over. Taking beautiful trips, redecorating your home or buying a new car … it can temporarily make you happy, but soon it feels normal again. The uplifting effect wears off, and only the next new thing can bring that hit of happiness you're looking for.

You can continue to buy new things or chase new experiences, but as long as you only change things on the *outside*, it won't make a lasting difference.

The ONLY thing that can deeply and permanently transform your life for the better is to make changes on the INSIDE. You need to clear the clutter from your mind, because the content of your mind—your beliefs, stories, convictions, expectations and everyday thoughts—is what determines your well-being and happiness. A mind filled with crappy thoughts results in a life that feels like crap. A mind filled with happy thoughts results in a happy life. That's a bit of a simplification, but at its core, it's true!

Some people don't know that their thoughts determine their happiness and well-being. Others know this already, but aren't able to turn that *knowing* into a *way of being and living*.

That's why I wrote this book. Because the ONLY way to create a happier, simpler and quieter life is to clear the clutter in your mind. To clean up or transform the thoughts, stories and beliefs that dampen your joy and make you feel stressed and overwhelmed.

In Part One of this book, I show you how your thoughts determine how you feel. I show you how your mind can make you feel like crap OR can make you feel on top of the world, regardless of the situation you're in. It may seem there's not much you can do about how you feel, but that's not true. When you change your mind, your life changes!

In Part Two, you receive practical tools and tips to clear your inner clutter and change your mind.

In Part Three, you learn the truth about yourself. You are not your mind. You are not your thoughts. And you're not only human. You're so much more than that! You are a soul having a human experience, a spark of the divine, a limitless being of light. You may already know that, but *knowing* this and *living in alignment* with that truth are two completely different things. That's what you learn in Part Four. As a result, an ocean of inner calm, peace and joy becomes available to you!

And finally, in Part Five, I share how I practice living in alignment with the truth of who I really am, a magnificent being of light in human form, which is exactly who you are, too! That sounds wonderful, but what good is knowing that when you need money to pay the rent or face other problems in life? I created five guidelines that help me with that and I share those with you in Part

Five. You'll also learn how to create your own guidelines and how you can work with them to simplify and upgrade your life.

I made all the information in this book easy to digest, to make it as simple, clear and clutter free as you'd like your mind to be. ;-)

Whatever it is you look for in your life: the ONLY place you can find it is INSIDE of yourself. And you can find it by using the power of your mind FOR you, instead of letting it bring you down or talk you out of your best ideas.

Your key to finding the happiness and well-being you desire is to clear the clutter that clogs up your mind and puts a layer of fog over your happiness and life.

Are you ready to clean your inner house, become an inner minimalist and access deep levels of well-being, happiness and joy?

Love,

Brigitte

THE RESULTS OF CLEARING YOUR MIND AND BECOMING AN INNER MINIMALIST

The title of this book promises a simpler, quieter, and happier life. That's definitely what you'll experience when you practice what you learn in this book. But those are not the only results you can expect. You will also gain more focus and energy. You'll feel calmer. Your power, joy, and sense of freedom will be enhanced. You'll be more creative, get more done in less time, experience better flow and receive more inspiration. Hearing your intuition will be easier. You'll worry less, experience less stress, and no longer feel overwhelmed.

Maybe you're already experienced in decluttering your mind or maybe this is fresh territory to you. No matter where you are on the journey of creating more clarity, calm, and joy in your life, I guarantee you there's even more to gain. There's no limit to how good life can get or how much joy, freedom, love, and happiness you can experience. But ... *clearing your mind takes practice*. It takes your focus, attention, and yes, it also involves some work. Just reading this book won't make much difference. You may feel uplifted and inspired, but if you don't implement what you learn, not much will change.

If you're *serious* about creating a simpler, quieter, and happier life, and want to enjoy the added side-bonuses I mentioned above, you need to *do* something with the content of this book. Start by making a commitment to yourself right here, right now. Promise yourself you won't just read the book, but you'll practice with what you learn, too. Set aside ten minutes a day to work on decluttering your mind and improving the quality of your thoughts—which will directly improve the quality of your results AND your life.

Are you willing to invest that time in your happiness? Are you willing to spend those ten minutes to reap the rewards in all areas of your business and life? Commit to it now and get excited about what becomes possible for you!!

YOUR COMMITMENT

I'm willing to invest ten minutes per day to practice what I learn so I can *vastly* increase my well-being and results!

PART ONE

ABOUT YOUR THOUGHTS

INTRODUCTION TO PART ONE

Before you learn how to clear your mind, it's important to understand how your thoughts impact your feelings and the results of your actions. Your thoughts affect *everything*. They shape and create your entire life!

The better you understand how much impact your thoughts have, the better you're able to transform and upgrade your thoughts. This automatically transforms and improves your entire life.

In this part of the book, I give you a quick tour of your mind. We look at the voices in your head, why your mind automatically turns to the negative, how your thoughts determine how you feel and more. Reading these chapters makes you aware of what goes on in your mind. You'll consciously notice what you're thinking, and this may give you a bit of a shock at first. As you start to pay more attention to your thoughts, you'll quickly learn how repetitive, negative and undermining they are.

Don't let that scare you off! See it as an invitation to keep reading and as proof that you're in the process of clearing your mind.

It's normal to freak out a little when you realize what goes on in your head, especially when exploring your thoughts and consciously working on your mindset is new to you. Remember that you're already thinking these thoughts and your mind is busy. The only thing that's changed is that you're now paying attention to it.

It's like the attic in your house that's filled to the brim with stuff. There are things you want to keep, hidden gems you forgot you had, and crap that needs to go. All these things are already there, but as long as you keep the door closed, you don't realize how much there is. Once you open the door and turn on the light, you realize how full it is. You can't see everything at once. Certain items catch your eye first. Before you can see what's hiding in the corners, you need to enter the attic and sort through the items. At first, this makes it even messier than before. But as you keep working through it, you'll end up with a clean and open space filled with treasures you can easily find.

Clearing the clutter in your mind is like that. What you do in part one of this book is take the first step: you climb up the attic, open the door, turn on the light and see what's there.

Don't let the cobwebs, the dust, or the mess scare you away. You're clearing it out, and you'll feel lighter soon!

So let's climb those stairs, open the door, and turn on the light, shall we?

Chapter 1
Your Thoughts Determine How You Feel

You may think that your circumstances determine how you feel. Or that your feelings show up out of nowhere. Even though it may *seem* that way, that's not how it works. Your thoughts determine how you feel. If you change your thoughts, your feelings change. We'll dive into how you can do that soon, but let's first look at how your thoughts determine your feelings.

Let's say you received an email from a potential client declining your offer. They've decided they will not work with you or purchase your service. The situation itself is neutral: you made an offer and your prospect turned it down. The meaning you attach to this event determines how this situation will make you feel.

When you think the rejection means that you can't pay your bills and might even go bankrupt, you'll feel scared and stressed. When you think this client's decision means you're a loser and no one wants to buy anything from you, you'll feel sad. When you think this outcome is a good thing because your schedule was too busy anyway, you'll probably feel relieved. When you think the world is filled with opportunities and missing out on this client means an even better deal will come your way, you'll feel excited about what's next. When your reaction is "whatever," you won't feel much about the potential client's decision at all.

Same situation. Different thoughts. Different feelings.

You can find peace in any situation. Yes, sometimes you experience big emotions that require time to grieve and heal. I'm not suggesting you can *think* your way out of those emotions. You need to *feel* your emotions in order to move through them. Sometimes you need to vent, cry, rage, or grieve. But even in those cases, the way you think about your situation determines how hard moving through your emotions will be. Thinking that all is lost and you'll never be happy again will make you feel worse than thinking that this too shall pass.

Your thoughts determine how you feel. Crappy thoughts, crappy life. Happy thoughts, happy life. Keep the constructive thoughts and upgrade or release the destructive ones, and your life will drastically improve. This book shows you how.

Pay more attention to your thoughts from now on. Notice what you think and how it makes you feel. Also notice how you feel and explore which thoughts caused you to feel this way.

If you don't believe that your thoughts determine your well-being, I invite you to open your mind. Just play with what you learn in this book and see if it makes a difference for you. Be curious and excited to see how your life can improve by changing your mind. Do you realize how wonderful that is? This means that YOU hold the power to your happiness—nothing and no one outside of you needs to change for you to feel better!

YOUR PRACTICE

Over the next couple of weeks, pay attention to how you feel in each moment. Notice your feelings and then explore what you're thinking. Which thoughts are generating which feelings?

Take notes of your findings. After a couple of days, you'll begin to see patterns and get insights into which thoughts typically bring you down or lift you up.

You'll probably also notice that your thoughts aren't unique. You think the same things, or variations on the same themes, over and over.

MINIMALIST MANTRAS*

- What I think determines what I feel.
- When I change my thoughts, I change the way I feel.
- Crappy thoughts, crappy life. Happy thoughts, happy life.

———

* These mantras are little reminders of the key points of each chapter. You can also use them as affirmations: write them in your journal or read them out loud. If one or more mantras resonate with you, read through them regularly. Consciously notice how reading each mantra makes you feel. Every time you read them it will shift something inside you. You can stop reading or reciting them when you notice you no longer need this reminder.

Chapter 2
Your Thoughts Impact Everything

In the previous chapter, we looked at how your thoughts determine how you feel. This impacts your life and outcomes in several ways.

One way your thoughts and feelings impact your outcomes is that they influence *what you do* or *how you do it*. If you feel scared about doing something, it increases the likelihood that you won't do it. If you don't believe it's possible to achieve your goals and dreams, it's likely you won't take actions that could help you realize them. This makes it harder or even impossible to make your dreams come true.

How you feel also determines *what you attract back to you*. If you've ever read anything about the Law of Attraction, you've heard this before: what you send out, you'll attract more of. When you ooze with joy, you'll see and experience more joy. When you ooze with failure, you'll see and experience more things that make you feel like a failure. Your feelings determine your energy. And as we've seen in the previous chapter: your thoughts determine how you feel.

The things you think about and focus on are what you'll see more of in your reality. Say you're thinking about buying a car. If you think about buying brand X, you suddenly see those cars everywhere. Not because they multiplied overnight, but because your focus is on them—and now you notice them wherever you go. If you're thinking about having a baby or are pregnant, you suddenly see pregnant women all around you. (Or so I'm told; I have no firsthand experience of this myself.)

What you focus on (or are preoccupied with) is what you'll see more of in your life. When most of your thoughts revolve around what's lacking and what's *not* working for you, you'll experience a feeling of deficiency and a feeling that things aren't working out. When you focus on what you DO have and what IS working, you'll see more and more evidence of it.

I recently noticed I was looking more at what's *not* working than at things that *are* working out for me. To help me shift my attention to things that *are* working, I write down ten pieces of evidence that things are going well for me every day. I added this to my daily journaling routine so it's easy to remember. I've only been doing it for two weeks and already notice a big difference in how I feel and what I focus on. I'll keep writing down daily evidence of things working out for me until looking on the bright side is my default state again.

Choose to focus on what you want to see *more* of instead of focusing on what you want to see less of. Whatever you look for, you will find. Choose to look for things you actually *want* to find. That's a surefire way to change your reality and outcomes of your actions and decisions.

YOUR PRACTICE

Pay attention to your recurring thoughts. What are you (unconsciously) focusing on? Are you thinking about what you want to see more of or what you want to see less of in your life?

Start looking for things you want to see more of. Look for what's working and what you already have. Look for evidence and signs that what you desire is unfolding in your life. Write it down in your journal. Feel grateful for it.

What you look for is what you will see. Start using this principle in your favor and notice the difference this makes in your life.

MINIMALIST MANTRAS

- My thoughts determine my results.
- What I look for and focus on is what I see and experience more of, so I make sure to focus on things I actually *want* to see more of in my life.
- The energy I send out attracts more energy on the same frequency.

CHAPTER 3

THE TRUTH ABOUT THOUGHTS

It can seem that your thoughts are stronger than you. They're not. Your thoughts have no power over you. You have power over *them*! Your thoughts only have as much power as you give them.

You are *not* your thoughts. They're just energy passing through, similar to clouds passing by in the sky.

You have the power to direct your thoughts in any direction you choose. You can train your mind to focus on constructive thoughts and not let your inner chatter take over. This takes practice and vigilance. It requires you to notice what you think and how this influences you. It requires you to learn how to change, release, and transform your thoughts. It requires you to learn how to shift focus without bypassing or suppressing your emotions.

Part Two of this book gives you several tools and tips to shift your state of being by clearing the clutter in your mind. For now, it's enough to know that you are not your thoughts. You're the person experiencing them. That's a big difference! Knowing this can bring relief and more inner peace. But it may not help enough. In that case, hang in there until you get to Part Two and can start slaying your unwanted musings. ;-)

MINIMALIST MANTRAS

- I am not my thoughts.
- I am the container that holds my thoughts.
- I have the power to direct my thoughts.

CHAPTER 4
WHY YOUR MIND AUTOMATICALLY TURNS TO THE NEGATIVE

Humans are wired with a fantastic survival instinct. Its job is to keep us alive and safe, and our instincts are always on the lookout for potential danger. When people lived in caves and were surrounded by predators, this was great. Back then, people were often exposed to potentially life-threatening experiences and they needed their brains to constantly scan their surroundings.

Since then, our environment and lifestyle have drastically changed. The survival instinct you inherited has not. It still scans your surroundings for danger. In the western world there aren't that many threats that could instantly kill you anymore. How often do you come face-to-face with a tiger or a snake?

But your brain is still alert. It has one simple rule: what you *know* is safe. What you don't know might not be. For that reason, your brain tries to keep you where you are, whether you like it there or not. It uses every trick in the book to keep you from wandering into unknown territory. That's why your thoughts tell you you'd better stay where you are and not take a risk. There could be danger lurking around every corner!

This is simplified and exaggerated, but my point is to show you that your brain, when left to its own devices, quickly turns to the negative. That's why it's important to remember two things. One, you can practice choosing what you focus on instead of letting your brain make up its own mind. And two, your mind is not doing this to bully or harm you. On the contrary: it's trying to keep you safe! Its intention is to help you, not harm you.

Don't curse your fears, your doubts, or your negative thoughts. They mean well. They have your best interest at heart. Thank them for their good work and let them know you intend to enter new territory anyway. Say, "Thank you for keeping me safe and thank you for warning me about a new situation. I hear you. And I'm stepping out of my comfort zone anyway. I've got this!"

MINIMALIST MANTRAS

- I'm in charge of my thoughts; my thoughts are not in charge of me.
- I can always change my mind.
- I decide what I focus on.

CHAPTER 5
NEGATIVE SELF-TALK

We all have an inner critic who tells us we're stupid, our ass looks fat in those jeans, or that article is too bad to publish. We all experience voices who tell us to shut up, hold back, play it safe, etcetera.

The primary messages these voices have for you is that you're either doing something wrong or that there's something wrong with you. These messages make you feel bad and they make it harder to pursue your dreams and do what you love.

These voices have nothing constructive to offer. They're mean, disrespectful, and unkind. You wouldn't dare talk to your loved ones that way! And you wouldn't let others talk to you this way, either. But when your own inner judge, censor, or critic raises its voice, you listen. You let it bring you down.

The keyword in that last sentence is *let*. That's the vital step to shutting those voices up. Remember: you are not your thoughts, and your thoughts have no more power over you than what you give them.

You don't have to listen to these voices. You don't have to give them power. You can tell them to shut up and instead give your power, focus, and attention to constructive thoughts that lift you up instead.

We'll explore how you can do that in Part Two. For now, just remember that these negative voices don't control you. You control them. It may not feel like it now, but you do. Even when you know how to shut them up, they still find ways to poison your mind. My inner critic is still very much alive and kicking! BUT it no longer has free rein like it used to. I know how to quickly shift my energy and mood, and sometimes, I even remember to do it. ;-) You're holding proof of that in your hands right now! If I'd listened to my inner critic, this book would not have been published. But I didn't listen to its negative voice. I chose to focus on the reasons why writing this book felt right.

MINIMALIST MANTRAS

- My thoughts have no more power over me than I give them.
- I don't allow negative self-talk to take up space in my mind.

Chapter 6
Not All Your Beliefs Are Yours

The message your negative self-talk has for you is rarely a message you came up with yourself. More often than not, it's a repetition of what you heard from others. The voice telling you that your ass is too fat is the voice of your bully in high school. The voice telling you that you should work harder if you want to amount to anything is the voice of your teacher.

Many of the beliefs and stories about yourself, which you take for granted, are not always messages you came up with yourself. Your beliefs about money are a hodgepodge collected from your parents, grandparents, teachers, friends, the news and media, and society. Your beliefs about how the world works come from those same sources. ALL your beliefs and ideas are at least *influenced* by others. You've heard the same things so often that you regard them as truth now. But that doesn't mean it's true at all. And it certainly doesn't mean that it's true for YOU.

What's true for one person can be a lie for you, and your truth can be a lie for another. A belief that works for others may actually hurt you.

For example, for me peanuts are a healthy treat. For others, this is a lie: when they eat even a part of a peanut, they could die. That peanut is not a healthy treat for them!

You need to have this same attitude toward your beliefs. You picked them up through others, and these beliefs may be true for them, but if they're true for YOU remains to be seen.

All your beliefs put together form the house you live in, so to speak. The quality of your beliefs determines if you feel like you live in a spacious castle or in a dark, narrow cage.

Questioning your beliefs is the beginning of breaking out of the cage of your thinking. Even a castle has room for expansion and more openness, freedom, and space!

We'll look at how you can dismantle the thoughts that don't support you in the next part of the book. For now, I want you to realize and remember that A) not all thoughts are your own and B) not everything you think or believe is true. Even when something is true for others, it might actually be *untrue* for *you*.

MINIMALIST MANTRAS

- What's true for others isn't necessarily true for me.
- Everyone has their own truth.
- Not everything I believe is true.

Chapter 7

Not Everything You Believe Is True

In the previous chapter you learned that not everything you believe is true. When you do believe something, this only means it is an often-repeated thought or a thought you never questioned before. That's all. Knowing this gives you two insight on how to transform your beliefs: by questioning your thoughts and by practicing thinking new thoughts.

Part Two gives you several tools that help you shift your thoughts and beliefs. For now, remember this: just because you believe something doesn't mean it's true. Even if every human being on the planet believes something doesn't mean it's true. Something that is true for your best friend doesn't mean it's true for you, and vice versa. Something that was true for you one year ago doesn't mean it's still true for you today.

Always be willing to question your thoughts and don't believe everything you think. It may be true, but often, it's not.

Minimalist Mantras

- A belief is only an often-repeated or unquestioned thought.
- I'm willing to question all my thoughts and beliefs.
- What if nothing I believe is true?

CHAPTER 8

THERE'S NO REASON TO FEAR YOUR THOUGHTS

The Law of Attraction tells us that thoughts become things: what you think about is what you'll attract in your life. As a result, people sometimes fear their thoughts. They're scared negative thoughts will put their dreams on hold or attract bad things into their life. THIS IS NOT TRUE.

There's no reason to fear your thoughts or worry that bad things will happen when you think about something bad. It can make you *feel* bad, sure, but that's about it.

The majority of your fears will NEVER be realized. Most things you think can go wrong never do. This shows you that NOT ALL thoughts become reality.

Does it help to consciously focus on what you want? Yes! Does it help to consciously focus on how you choose to feel? Yes! Doing this helps you feel better and calmer and helps you to enjoy life more. Practicing thinking this way helps you attract what you want and makes it easier to manifest your desires.

But if you don't feel good, or you are sad or hurt, good things can STILL happen for you. You can't mess up your life by feeling down or thinking "bad" thoughts. Those are a part of being human. They're part of life. There's nothing wrong with it and there's nothing wrong with you.

Focus on the positive but NEVER deny the negative. Suppressing or bypassing the negative thoughts hurts you more than feeling your bad feelings could ever do.

Think about what you want, feel what you feel. NEVER suppress your emotions and don't worry about "bad" or "negative" thoughts. The best way to deal with them is NOT to deny they exist. The best way to deal with your thoughts and emotions is to acknowledge them, feel them, process them in any way you need, and then consciously choose to not give your power away to them. Explore if there's something you could do to feel better, if only a little. All the tools in this book help you with that.

MINIMALIST MANTRAS

- There's no reason to fear my thoughts.
- There are no "bad" thoughts or feelings. There are simply thoughts and feelings.
- I allow myself to think what I think and to feel what I feel.

PART TWO

HOW TO CLEAR THE CLUTTER FROM YOUR MIND

INTRODUCTION TO PART TWO

In Part One you learned that your thoughts have no power over you. Not everything you believe is true and not all your thoughts and beliefs are yours.

In this part of the book we move on to the juicy part: how to dismantle negative thoughts, tell your inner voices to shut up, and clear the clutter from your mind. Yay!

You may already know a lot about shifting and dismantling your thoughts and beliefs, or you may be a total newbie at this. No matter what you already know or how good you already are at feeling calm, joyful, happy and at peace, there's always space for improvement. There's always room for more joy, happiness, inner freedom, calm, and peace. There's always room for more life!

Chapter 1
Five Steps to Clear Your Mind

The basic steps to clear your mind are always the same, regardless of what tool you use.

STEP ONE: NOTICE HOW YOU FEEL

Pay attention to how you feel. Do you often rush through your days and jump from one activity to the next without taking the time to check in with yourself? When you don't feel good, do you often push through it, trying to ignore it or distract yourself from it? When you feel bad, this feeling can take over and color your mood for the rest of the day. You may even end up in a downward spiral that makes you feel worse and worse.

Don't live around your feelings. *Consciously notice how you feel.*

STEP TWO: STAY WITH THE FEELING

Your first response to not feeling well is to move away from it. Don't. Move toward it instead. Explore. Be curious and open. Ask yourself, "I wonder what I'm thinking that makes me feel this way?!"

Remember, it's your *thinking* that makes you feel bad. Not the situation you're in. Not your environment, the economy, politics, the state of the world, or your bank account. No. It's what you *think about* those things that makes you feel the way you do. You can change the way you feel by changing what you think.

STEP THREE: UNCOVER AND WRITE DOWN YOUR THOUGHTS

Take out your journal and write down your thoughts. What's going through your mind? Write it all down. When you explore what's in your head, your mind will keep spinning. You need to put your thoughts onto paper so you can work with them.

Sometimes noticing your thoughts is enough to shift your mood. If that doesn't happen automatically, move on to step four.

STEP FOUR: DO YOU REALLY BELIEVE THIS?

Examine each thought you have individually. Do you *really* believe this? Are you 100% certain that this is the absolute truth, always?

When your answer is *no*, this thought is eliminated and loses its power.

When your answer is *maybe*, you've created space between your thoughts and yourself. The space allows you to loosen the grip this thought has on you, and you can transform or release it. (More on how to do this soon.)

When your answer is *yes*, ask yourself how you benefit from holding on to this thought. How does believing this serve you? How does it empower you and make you feel better? If it doesn't serve you, what would you like to believe instead? What would improve your mood? What would make you feel more powerful? What new thought would give you more hope? Notice what comes up and how these new thoughts make you feel.

Ask yourself if something else could also be true. Is there another way to look at this thought that will make you feel better, if only a little? See what comes up and write it all down.

Often, taking these four steps is all it takes to lift your spirits. Sometimes you need more, or you want to feel even better. That's where step five comes in.

STEP FIVE: SHIFT YOUR THINKING

In the following chapters, I'll give you tools to help you to weed out crappy thoughts and replace them with better ones. Use these tools and remember: crappy thoughts, crappy life; happy thoughts, happy life. Your thoughts don't just happen to you, leaving you powerless and at their mercy. You can *always* train your mind and shift your thoughts. The more you practice, the easier it will be, the quicker you'll shift out of bad moods, the clearer your mind becomes AND … the more your mind will turn to better quality thoughts, all by itself! Your whole mindset improves when you clear your inner clutter.

Before we dive into tools to shift your thoughts, I want to share one more example that shows how your thoughts determine your feelings. In 2003, I was at a workshop given by Byron Katie, and she shared a story that beautifully illustrates the impact your thoughts have on your emotions.

Imagine that you're walking in a lovely forest. The sun is shining, birds are tweeting, a soft breeze strokes your skin, everything is perfect and you feel happy and relaxed.

Suddenly you see a snake a couple of feet in front of you. Oh no! Your heart pounds, you start to sweat, panic takes over, and all your systems are on high alert.

Now what? You don't want to walk back. You're afraid to walk past the snake. You also don't want to leave the trail and get lost in the woods. Very carefully, you take a couple of steps forward. Now that you're closer, you suddenly see what it is. It's not a snake. It's a piece of rope …

You sigh, then burst out laughing. Your heart rate drops. Your breathing goes back to normal. You walk on. In no time, you feel as happy and relaxed as you did before.

What changed? Not your environment. Not what you're doing. The only thing that changed were your *thoughts*.

When you thought you saw a snake, you freaked out and your entire system was preparing for flight. The moment you saw it was a piece of rope, you automatically calmed down.

When your mind changes, everything changes. This is how it always works. When your thoughts change, your reality changes. When you change on the inside, the outside changes, too.

IMPORTANT REMINDER

It's NEVER a good idea to bypass or suppress your emotions. Yes, shifting your thoughts changes how you feel. But rationalizing your feelings away isn't good for you. Unfelt emotions fester underneath fake positive thinking. If you need to vent, cry, grieve, or be angry by all means, do that! Allow yourself to feel *all* your emotions and *never* suppress them. Let your emotions out in whatever ways feel natural and don't hurt you or others. Move on to shifting your thoughts only *after* you have felt your way through your emotions.

YOUR PRACTICE

Pay more attention to how you feel. Take a moment in the morning, and periodically throughout the day, to stop what you're doing and check in with yourself. How do you feel? What's going on inside you? What would make you feel (even) better now?

MINIMALIST MANTRAS

- My thoughts don't just happen to me, I can train my mind and shift my thoughts, always.
- I allow myself to feel what I feel and to express my emotions instead of suppressing them.

CHAPTER 2

HOW YOU KNOW WHICH THOUGHTS TO CLEAR

Have you heard of Marie Kondo*? She's an expert at organizing and helps people clear the clutter from their homes. To help people decide which items to throw away and which items to keep, she has a simple rule: an item that sparks joy can stay. If it doesn't, it needs to go.

You can apply that same principle to your thoughts. A thought that sparks joy can stay, a thought that doesn't needs to go (or be transformed). What remains is a clear, calm mind.

Here's an example of how you can work with this principle.

Start the day by exploring how you feel and what you think. How your day begins makes a tremendous difference in how you feel throughout the day. When you feel busy and rushed in the morning, you'll feel busy and rushed all day—IF you do nothing to clear your mind. When you take a moment to tend to your inner household, you'll feel calmer and more energized throughout the day.

Take out your journal and answer this question first: how do I feel? Write down everything that comes up. You can also describe where in your body you feel your feelings. When you feel stressed,

---

* Marie Kondo is the author of the book: *The Life-Changing Magic of Tidying: A simple, effective way to banish clutter forever.*

can you feel tension in your shoulders or jaw? Or can you feel a lump in your stomach?

Once you find *where* you feel stress, ask yourself what you're thinking. Which thoughts are going through your mind? What do you think about yourself, your life, the day ahead? Which thoughts made you feel the way you do? Write them all down.

This practice shows you which thoughts lift you up, and which ones bring you down. This practice also gives you clarity in the thoughts you can shift or release. You learn how to do that in the following chapters.

YOUR PRACTICE

For at least one week (preferably longer to benefit from this practice even more), start your day with journaling.

Ask yourself: how do I feel? Write your answer in your journal or notebook. Then ask yourself: what am I thinking now or what was I just thinking about? These are the thoughts that caused you to feel the way you do.

You can also write these notes on your computer or in your phone. However, writing by hand offers benefits typing doesn't. Writing by hand slows you down and helps you explore your inner world on a deeper level. It also helps you process your thoughts better.

TIP

Do this exercise *every time* you notice you don't feel good. Write down your thoughts when you feel worried, stressed out, overwhelmed, angry, or sad. If you don't have time to write it down or hate journaling, record it on your phone. What do you feel? What did you think that made you feel that way?

You may feel that you don't have the time to do this, but it MASSIVELY pays off when you *make* the time to do this. In the long run, it saves you energy when you look at your feelings instead of ignoring or suppressing them. Making time to express your thoughts gives you more space and often instantly calms your mind. When you clear your unconstructive thoughts using one of the tools in the following chapters, you'll be happier and be more efficient afterward.

I did this exercise myself while I was editing this chapter. It felt like a chore and I was not enjoying it. So I stopped and asked myself what was off. The thoughts going through my mind were bringing me down. They told me that my book sucked and there was no point in editing because the book wasn't good enough to be published. I recognized these thoughts for what they were: a part of the creative cycle you always go through when you write a book. (Or create anything, really.) One moment you're excited and think your book is great, the next you think your book (and you) are a total failure. I know this cycle intimately and know that none of these thoughts say anything about the quality of the book. Reminding myself of this was enough to shake off those negative voices and continue to edit. With joy this time. ;-) I felt so much better and moved forward quicker—all because I took a couple of minutes to explore what was going on in my head.

MINIMALIST MANTRAS

- A thought that sparks joy can stay, a thought that doesn't needs to go.
- When I don't feel good, I know it's time to explore what I think and to question what I believe.

CHAPTER 3
BRAIN DUMP

Another way to clear your mind at the beginning of your day is to do a brain dump: take out your journal and for ten minutes, write down *everything* that comes up *exactly* as it comes up.

You'll notice your mind goes all over the place. You think about your grocery list and what to have for dinner; you remind yourself to send a birthday card and to pick up your dry cleaning. You think about the strange dream you had, what the name of that singer is, if he's still alive, and if you should see a doctor about that spot on your back. All this can go through your mind in a couple of seconds!

If you jump into your day with this frazzled mind, you'll feel frazzled, too. You'll react to your to-do list and whatever crosses your path—instead of calmly working on the things that matter with a clear, focused mind.

So dump that clutter onto paper just like you take out the garbage. You don't have to analyze anything you write down. Just dump it. Better out than in!

If writing down your thoughts is ALL you do, this will change how you feel and quickly make a positive difference. Your mind will definitely feel clearer after you do this exercise! Try it in the morning (and whenever you're drowning in a whirlwind of thoughts).

If you need more tools to calm your mind down, the following chapters help. Choose the one that speaks to you and practice with it regularly.

MINIMALIST MANTRA

- A great way to clear my mind is to dump my thoughts on paper. This clears my mind like taking out the trash clears my home.

Chapter 4
Dismantle Negative Self-Talk

Here's a beautiful way to dismantle a negative thought. First, write it down. Then write down the opposite of this negative thought. Finally, find one to three examples that show you this positive thought is already true. For example, you notice yourself thinking a thought like "Oh, I'm so stupid." STOP. Write down "I'm stupid" and then write down the opposite of that. Let's say you pick "smart." Write down "I'm smart." Now, come up with one to three examples (more is okay!) that prove you are smart. Maybe you made the right decision about an investment; maybe you handled a tricky situation well, maybe you graduated with great grades. It doesn't matter how long ago it happened, it all counts as evidence.

I guarantee you will always find examples! Why? Because multiple truths exist at the same time. If you look for examples of making a mistake, you will find them. If you look for examples of doing something right, you will find them. What you look for is what you will find. Always!

Don't look for examples that prove you're stupid!!! You don't need any further reasons to criticize yourself. Most people have an overly active inner critic and chances are, yours keeps herself pretty busy, too. You want your inner critic to back off. That's what this exercise does.

If you have several negative thoughts you repeatedly think about yourself, write them all down. Write the positive opposite of each thought next to it. Find one to three examples that prove this positive statement about yourself is already true.

Finally, you can play with this exercise daily by writing down evidence that your positive thought about yourself (or others, life, or the world) is already true.

MINIMALIST MANTRAS

- I have the power to choose how I think about myself.
- I have the power to change how I think about everything.
- I choose to think only kind thoughts about myself.

Chapter 5
What is Possible?

There's only one reason people hold on to a belief, and that's that it serves them on some level. As long as a part of you thinks you will benefit from holding on to a belief, you won't be able to transform it or let it go.

The way to change this is to ask yourself these three questions.

- How does holding on to this belief benefit you?
- What is possible if you no longer believed this?
- What (new) belief serves you better?

Let's say you have an idea for a workshop. But the last time you offered one, no one signed up. So now, your excitement for this idea is quickly overshadowed by the thought that there's no point in creating a new workshop because no one will sign up. Again.

What's the benefit of holding on to the belief that there's no point to create a new workshop? If you believe there's no point, you don't offer the workshop. If you don't offer it, you can't fail and you can't be disappointed. You won't have to go through the experience of no one signing up for your workshop again.

Now, think about the possibilities.

Once you've stopped believing that there's no point to create a new workshop, what would be possible? You'd create it. You'd have a chance to succeed. You could experience what it feels like to deliver a great workshop.

What (new) belief serves you better?

You never know what might happen. It could work out this time!

Asking yourself these three questions helps you let go of beliefs that are holding you back. Look at your belief from all angles and notice the thoughts that help you or hinder you. Now, you're free to make a conscious decision about what you believe. This is a great way to clear your mind of limiting thoughts and perspectives.

MINIMALIST MANTRAS

- I have no idea what's possible for me.
- I have no idea how good things can get!
- I have no idea how well everything can work out for me.

Chapter 6

Who Would You Be Without This Thought?

After you notice how you feel and write down what you think, take a good look at the effect of each thought. Take your time to feel into your answers as you write everything down. Noticing the impact your thoughts have on your well-being helps you release thoughts that no longer serve you—they can fall away once you clearly see their effect on you. Your mood shifts and your mind will feel clearer as a result of doing this exercise. For each thought you write down, answer the questions.

- How do you feel when you believe this?
- How does that affect what you do? How does believing this thought impact your behavior? What effect does that have on your life? What effect does that have on your business or work?
- How would you feel if you did *not* believe this?
- How would *not* believing this affect what you do? How would it impact your behavior? What effect would that have on your life? What effect would that have on your business or work?

Notice how you feel before and after you've answered these questions. How do you feel different?

You may find it hard to come up with answers for all questions. That's okay. Whatever comes up helps to increase your awareness of the effect of your thoughts and makes it easier to shift into thinking more supporting thoughts.

Here's an example to show you what doing this exercise can look like.

Thought: I don't have enough time every day.

1. *How do I feel when I believe this?* I feel stressed.

2. *How does it affect what I do?* It causes me to be cranky, and it causes me to lose focus.

3. *How does believing this thought impact my behavior?* Because I don't feel like I have enough time, I get up early and I stay up late, I don't take breaks or get enough exercise.

What effect does that have on my life? I'm more tired, more cranky. Every item on my already long to-do list feels too heavy to shift. I'm not sleeping well or getting enough rest, so I don't work well the next day.

What effect does that have on my business or work? It's harder to concentrate and focus. It's harder to deliver good work. I enjoy my work less.

4. *How would I feel if I didn't believe this?* I would feel less stressed and less cranky.

5. *How would not believing this affect what I do?* Maybe if I worried less about not having enough time, the space / time I spend worrying will be freed up for me to focus on my to-do list.

How would it impact my behavior? I wouldn't think about everything I have to do all the time. I'd take time to relax or exercise even when my work wasn't finished.

What effect would that have on my life? I'd feel happier and less stressed. I'd sleep better.

What effect would that have on my business or work? I'd be able to focus more on my work. I'd probably also get more work done.

Once you see the effect this thought has on you and what could open up if you no longer believed it, you can come up with a new thought that will serve you better. The next chapter shows you how to do this.

MINIMALIST MANTRAS

- I choose my thoughts wisely.
- I choose what I believe.

Chapter 7
What Else Could Be True?

After you notice how you feel and after you write down your thoughts, you can find new thoughts that will make you feel better. Look at the list of your thoughts and identify the one that hurts the most. Can't choose between one or more hurtful thoughts? Pick a random one to work with first.

Ask "What else could be true?" and come up with a different thought that you believe AND that makes you feel better, even if only slightly.

Ask and answer that same question again and come up with a new thought you believe that makes you feel better. Repeat until you can't come up with an even better thought.

If necessary, go through this process for the next hurtful thought. Often you won't need to because your mood has already drastically improved.

Let's first look at the stressful thought from the previous chapter: I don't have enough time every day. A new thought you believe and that makes you feel better could be: I only have to focus on one task at a time.

Here's another example to show you what this process looks like. Let's say you felt bad because a client said no to your proposal. You explored what you were thinking and uncovered these thoughts:

- I completely messed up. I'm a failure.
- OMG, how am I ever going to pay my bills next month!
- Everything is lost.
- I'm a lousy entrepreneur and I'll never make it.
- I'll never find another client in this economy.

The thought that hurts you most is *I'll never find another client in this economy.* A new thought you believe AND makes you feel better could be *People spend money in any economy.*

Next come up with a new belief that will improve your mood:

If people spend money in any economy, I can sell something in any economy.

Continue to come up with new thoughts that make you feel better AND that you believe: I only need one new client to make enough money to pay my bills next month.

Of all the millions of people in the country, I only have to find ONE person to buy something from me.

Of course I'll find a new client! There are plenty of opportunities for me, always.

If you can't think of anything better or your mood has improved and your mind is calm and clear again, you're done!

MINIMALIST MANTRAS

- I can always find multiple truths in every situation.
- There's never just ONE truth or perspective—I can look at situations from multiple angles and choose the perspective that serves me the most.

CHAPTER 8
MIND YOUR WORDS

While you are learning to be mindful of how you think, it's a good reminder to be mindful of how you talk. How do you talk about your past, yourself, your business, your dreams, your memories, your life? What stories do you repeat, and how do you tell them?

Your words shape your world. They have creative power. They determine how you feel. They determine your entire life.

Pay attention to your words like never before. Choose words that make you feel good. The moment you say something that triggers feelings of doubt, hopelessness, helplessness or fear, *change your words*. Choose a different perspective. It's a simple way to keep your mind clear and feel better. Not easy, mind you! It takes practice and constant awareness. It's rewarding, though, because it instantly makes a difference.

Here are some tips and examples to help you choose your language wisely and constructively.

Talk about possibilities:
Replace: "I can't get a new job because of the shitty economy."
With: "I might get a new job. You never know!"
Or with: "I'm curious to see what job I could find!"
Or with: "I only need one job, that's doable in any economy!"

Replace: "I can't afford that."
With: "I'll see how I can come up with the money for it."
Or with: "I'm going to save for it!"
Or with: "I choose to spend my money on something different now."

Replace: "That's not possible."
With: "I wonder what *could* be possible. What other options might there be?"
Or with: "I wonder how it might work out for me?"
Or with: "You never know. Stranger things have happened. Miracles happen every day!"

Replace: "That was so stupid of me!"
With: "From now on, I'll do this instead."

Replace: "I'm stuck."
With: "I'm not sure what to do now, but that's okay. Answers will come to me somehow."

Pay attention to how you talk about painful memories and experiences:
When you focus on pain, loss, shame or disappointment, you keep the painful emotions alive. You bring the pain into your present experience. But it already happened. It's done. If you still need to vent or heal, of course, do that! I'm not suggesting suppressing or denying your emotions. Vent, cry, grieve, and heal as much as you need. AND … start to tell a different story. Change your thoughts and change your words. Choose language that focuses on closure. Language that makes it clear this was the past, or words that show what you've learned from your experience.
For example, replace: "I did some embarrassing things in the past."
With: "I'm the only one who remembers that. If they can forget it, so can I."

Replace: "Since I've always been this way, I'll never change."
With: "I can't change who I was, but I can change who I will be today."

Focus on the bright side, the positive, or on something neutral:
Replace: "I hate being stuck in traffic and now I'll be late!"
With: "Ah well, nothing I can do about it now. How can I enjoy this extra 'me' time?"

Replace: "I don't know how to get through this!"
With: "I'm sure this too shall pass (even though it doesn't feel like it now)."

Replace: "I don't know how to do this!"
With: "I can learn how this works or find someone to help me with it."

Replace: "My dream still hasn't come true!"
With: "I'm in the process of achieving this."

Pay attention to your thoughts and words. Notice if your self-talk makes you feel bad and is destructive and unsupportive. Be aware of how your words make you feel. Consciously choose different words if you don't feel good.

If you like, you can ask a friend to support you. Ask them to point it out when you talk in negative ways about yourself (or anything, really).

MINIMALIST MANTRAS

- My words create my world, so I choose them carefully.
- I'm mindful of the words I use and choose the words that make me feel best.

CHAPTER 9
REST YOUR MIND

Literally give it a rest. Don't read. Don't watch television. Don't talk. Don't work. Don't mindlessly wander down the rabbit hole that is the internet.

Do *nothing*. Stare at the sky, the clouds, the water, your pet. Pick your nose. Repeat a mantra. Listen to soothing music. Take a walk. Listen to your breath. Sip your tea. Meditate. Ask to be left alone for a while or go into another room and close the door. Just BE.

Repeat daily for at least a couple of minutes.

When you first practice this, it may *seem* that your mind becomes busier than ever. It doesn't. You just consciously notice how busy it has always been in there. All the more reason to give your mind a break!

This does NOT mean that you should focus on not thinking. That will never happen! What it means is that you don't put your mind to work. Use one of the suggestions I mentioned above. Or do yoga or a workout. Working your body relaxes your brain, too.

MINIMALIST MANTRAS

- I regularly give my mind a break.
- A rested mind is a clear mind.

Chapter 10
Recognize Your Truth

Do you know what's true for you? Do you know what's best for you and works for you? When your thoughts and actions are in line with your truth, you feel good. When they're not, you don't. That's why it's important to know your truths and act accordingly. You can't feel happy when you betray yourself!

It's not always possible to *think* your way to your truth. You can get trapped in conflicting thoughts, and fears and doubts can show up, too. It's better to *feel* your way to your truth instead. Here are the signs to pay attention to.

Possible signs that something is NOT true for you.

- It makes you feel heavier.
- It doesn't feel good.
- It makes you feel restless.
- It contracts you.
- You feel tension in your body.
- You can find it harder to breathe. You clench your jaws.

When you connect with your truth, it feels quite different.

- It makes you feel lighter and calmer.

- It expands you.
- It opens you up.
- You experience more space and freedom in your body and mind.
- Your shoulders (and body) relax.

It may take some practice to learn to feel your way to your truth. Something that helps to build awareness is to pay more attention to your body. Notice how your body feels when you're relaxed. Notice how your body feels when you're stressed, worried, overwhelmed, or scared. Note how you feel when you speak your truth and how you feel when you swallow your words. Pay attention to how you feel when you do something you *want* to do and how it feels when you do something you *don't* want to do.

When you do this, you get to know your body. You learn how it communicates with you and guides you. You inhabit your body more, which automatically takes you out of the busyness of your head. You'll learn to recognize the faintest signs that something is right or wrong for you. Your body always knows. Your body always tells you. You don't need your head to figure out what's best for you. When you listen to your body, you always *know*.

When something isn't right for me, for example, I feel this as a knot in my stomach. When I'm stressed, I feel my shoulders tense up. When something is true and I'm on the right track, I feel goosebumps all over.

YOUR PRACTICE

Pay more attention to your body. Notice what you feel and how your body reacts at different times under different situations and circumstances.

MINIMALIST MANTRAS

- My body always knows what's true for me.
- My body is always communicating with me, and I intend to listen to her from now on!

CHAPTER 11
GROUNDED AND CENTERED

Many (western) people don't live from their heart. They live from (and in) their head. When you live in your head, you *think* your way through life instead of actually *living* it. You think too much. You're not calm. You're not grounded in your body, in your inner wisdom, in your intuition, or in your heart.

When you're grounded and centered in your body, you're automatically connected with your heart. You feel what's right for you. You're open to the guidance of your intuition. You're present and at peace. This frees up your mind so it can optimally serve you instead of hinder you with unproductive thoughts. Calm, peace, and more inner quiet are the result. You feel more at home in your body and your mind stops overworking and overthinking.

Grounding and centering yourself is easy. You can do it physically by breathing deep into your belly. This brings your attention to the center of your body, just below your navel. When you're centered, you literally stand more firmly on the ground. (This is why in all martial arts, grounding and centering yourself is key.) You're connected to your inner power and strength and feel stable and secure.

You can ground yourself by jumping up and down a couple of times. Try it and notice how you "sink" into your legs more.

Or bring your attention to your feet and consciously feel every movement your feet make when you walk.

You can also ground yourself energetically* by imagining little roots shooting from the soles of your feet into the earth, growing strong like the roots of an ancient tree.

When you're grounded and centered, you're open to receive the wisdom of your heart. You feel it in hunches, a sudden knowing, a bodily sensation. You just *know*.

Your soul guides you every second of every day. The more grounded and present you are, the easier it is to receive the wisdom your heart, body, and soul always share with you. Your soul never guides you wrong.

Your mind can take you off track by steering you in directions based on fears, lies and lack. Your heart and soul never do that. They guide you based on love, truth, and abundance.

The more you live in your head, the more fears, overwhelm, worry, and stress you can experience. The less you live in your head, the more love, calm, peace, and happiness you experience.

I know that I'm in my head when I'm restless and anxious. Or when I think that I need to figure things out or I'm not sure how to do something. For me, thoughts like these and / or feeling stressed are surefire signs I'm in my head and not present in this moment.

How can you recognize that you're ungrounded and in your head?

MINIMALIST MANTRAS

- My soul guides me every second of every day.
- My intuition never steers me wrong.
- I live from my heart and follow my intuition and joy.

---

* Finding it difficult to ground and center yourself? Sign up for bonus gifts at www.innerminimalistgifts.com and receive a short audio file that helps you ground, center, and deeply connect to your heart, body, and soul.

Chapter 12
Acceptance

You may not like your current experience or a certain situation in your life, but in this moment, it is what it is. You can fight, resist, or dislike it all you want but right now, *it is what it is*.

Fighting what *is* takes a lot of energy. It's a waste of energy, too. What you resist persists.

If you want to save energy, feel calmer, and be able to change your situation, it helps to embrace and accept *everything* in your life. That doesn't mean you have to like it. It doesn't mean you give up on yourself or your dreams, and it doesn't mean that you will always stay where you are. That's not what acceptance means. It means that you accept that *in this moment*, things are the way they are. You *can* change it and it *will* change, but right now, this is it.

When you practice acceptance, you'll feel calmer. It brings you relief. It takes up so much time and energy to fight and resist. You don't even know how much time and energy you are using until you stop doing it!

While I was writing this chapter, my neighbors were doing god knows what, but it made a hell of a lot of noise, making it hard for me to concentrate on my writing. I fought that noise like crazy. I kept thinking how much I HATE noise and how I wished for it to be quiet. Then I realized I was doing EXACTLY what I'm telling you *not* to do in this chapter. I was fighting what was happening. So I stopped doing it. I accepted that in this moment, it was not quiet. It was noisy, and I didn't like it. I accepted it ALL: the noise, disliking it, resisting it, and wanting it to be gone. I accepted it unconditionally, knowing that my resistance *could not change or improve the situation or how I felt.* On the contrary, my resistance made me feel worse. Because now, it was noisy outside AND inside of me!

I couldn't change the noise. But I could change my response. Resistance was my knee-jerk reaction. Accepting the situation and all my thoughts and feelings around it was a conscious decision, one that instantly calmed me down, even though the neighbors were still loud.

The more you accept the way things are, the calmer and more at peace you feel. It saves you a lot of energy and time, and most importantly, it clears the path to change. You can't always change the situation, but you can ALWAYS change your perspective on it and how you respond to it.

And now I'm at the end of this chapter, I suddenly realized the noise stopped at some point—and I didn't even notice. Letting go of my resistance helped me forget about the noise somehow, so I was free to focus on my writing.

MINIMALIST MANTRAS

- The more I accept the way things are, the easier it is to change the way things are.
- I can't always change the situation, but I can always change how I look at and respond to it.
- The more I accept the way things are, the calmer I feel.
- The only fight you ever have is with yourself.

Chapter 13
Feel Instead of Think

When you feel overwhelmed, worried, fearful or stressed, you should explore your thoughts and shift the ones that make you feel that way. The previous chapters gave you several tools that help you with this.

But sometimes exploring your thoughts doesn't work. Or you don't feel like exploring your thoughts. What you can do instead is to *feel* everything that goes on inside you, without labeling, judging, or thinking anything about what you experience or think. Without trying to solve anything. Without suppressing your feelings or trying to make them go away. Just FEEL what you feel. BE with your emotions and the sensations in your body. *Where* do you feel it in your body? *What* do you feel in your body?

See if you can breathe to it. Imagine that when you breathe in, oxygen flows to a specific place in your body, and that it fills up that spot. When you breathe out, imagine that this empties from that spot so the tension there can leave your body.

Everything is energy, *including* your emotions, tension, and stress. Energy *can* and *will* flow again when you let it. By doing this, your feelings let go of you instead of the other way around.

So just feel. Breathe. BE. All is well. You're experiencing emotions and feel them in your body. It may be uncomfortable, but stay with it. When you allow every feeling to be there, every feeling will gently move away.

Keep your focus on what you feel in your body. If you want to think about anything, think about ways to describe what you feel. DO NOT think about the issue, how to solve it, or the story you spun around your situation. It's these thoughts that keep you trapped and make you feel bad.

Allow yourself to feel it all, allow every feeling to be there, keep breathing and keep noticing what you sense in your body. Eventually all your stress, fears, worries, and doubts will flow out of you.

It can be difficult to practice this when you're in the middle of a full-blown emotional shitstorm. So practice *being* with your feelings. Practice noticing everything that goes on inside and around you in moments where not much is going on, like right now. What do you feel in your body? Where do you feel it? Does it have a shape, a color, a smell? What kind of sensation is it? Imagine that when you breathe in, your breath travels to a place in your body where you feel tension or pain. Does anything change when you do that? Notice. Feel. Breathe. BE. Doing this takes you out of your head and into your body. It quiets your mind and helps you release stress and unrest.

MINIMALIST MANTRAS

- I allow myself to feel all my feelings.
- I allow myself to express all my feelings.
- I'm not afraid of my feelings or emotions.

CHAPTER 14
RESPONSIBLE

You're *only* in charge of and responsible for things that are your business: your actions, thoughts, feelings, results, perspective, etcetera. You can't control what others do, feel, think, or achieve. You can't control what they believe or how they react. You can't control the universe either. You can try, but it's a lost cause. Trying to control it is a big energy drain and clouds your mind.

Focus on what you *can* change and what you have full control over: YOURSELF and your thoughts, habits, perspectives, responses, actions and reactions. And let go of everything else. Stop trying to make others or the universe bend to your will. The more you stop trying to control what's out of your reach, the more inner peace and calm you'll experience. The more energy you have, the more power you have access to.

This afternoon I sent an email to pitch one of my books to a podcast. It's a super cool podcast and I'd love be a guest! But I can't control that. The only thing I *have* control over is the copy of my email, when I send it, when I'll send a follow up email and what I will write in that email. I have no control over how the reader will react or if they'll invite me for an interview.

I'm not responsible for their response and I certainly can't control it. I give the things I *can* control my full attention and love, and then let go of any attachment or expectation.

MINIMALIST MANTRAS

- I take full responsibility for everything I'm responsible for.
- I let go of all responsibilities that aren't mine.
- I focus on what I can control instead of trying to change what I can't influence.

CHAPTER 15
STOP IT

Did you ever see the clip called "Stop It" with comedian Bob Newhart? In it, you see a woman talking to her psychologist, played by Newhart. She tells him about a fear she has and how every time she thinks about it she panics. Newhart has a solution for that: just stop thinking about it! It's a funny video. (Google it! Even though you know what happens, you'll still laugh.) AND … it really works!

One tool that helps you snap out of a train of thoughts is to come up with a short sentence you repeat when you notice the thoughts creeping up. It can be "stop it" or something else.

A sentence that helps me step out of shitty thoughts is: "And the good news is …" This sentence works wonders when I'm caught up in thoughts like: "I have to go to the dentist. Oh no, I *hate* that! It's scary and I don't like it and … and the good news is: I still have all my teeth! And I have enough money to pay for the dentist!"

If this sentence speaks to you, use it. Or try "This too shall pass." Or come up with another expression. It can be anything. All it has to do is cut through your thoughts so they no longer have a hold on you.

Another idea of something you can do to stop a train of thoughts is to snap your fingers. Just play with it and see what works for you. Anything that helps you stop going around in circles and driving yourself crazy is wonderful.

MINIMALIST MANTRAS

- I can easily snap out of any thought or emotion.
- My thoughts don't have a hold on me. I can snap out of them in an instant.

CHAPTER 16
TRANSCEND YOUR THOUGHTS

Instead of exploring and shifting your thoughts, you can also transcend them. You rise above your thoughts by shifting your attention from what you *think* to what you *feel*. Here's how it works. When you notice you don't feel good, notice what you're feeling. Then ask yourself how you want to feel instead. You know what you don't want to feel, but how DO you want to feel? Then *feel* that feeling now.

Let's say you feel overwhelmed and want to feel calm instead. Imagine how it would feel to experience calm now. Is there a part of your body where you feel calm? Bring your attention to that part of your body. If that doesn't work, can you come up with a memory of a time you felt at peace? Can you relive that memory now?

If that doesn't work, ask yourself what would help you calm down. Maybe there's music you can listen to. Maybe a walk would help. Do what you need to do to feel how you want to feel.

I used this strategy recently when I felt restless without any apparent reason. Thinking about why I felt restless didn't give me any insights, and it was obvious that thinking about this more would not make me feel any different. So I asked myself how I wanted to feel instead. Relaxed, was the answer that immediately came up. I was too restless to come up with a memory of a time I felt relaxed, so I chose to listen to a guided meditation that helped me feel more peaceful instead. It worked like a charm!

It's not always possible to focus on experiencing a different feeling. Sometimes you need to let your emotions out first. Do that if that's what you need.

Sometimes it feels impossible to access the feeling you're looking for. When that's the case, use one of the other tools in this book. What will probably work better now is grounding yourself (Part Two, *Chapter 11: Grounded and Centered)* or bring yourself back to this moment, your body and your breath (Part Four, *Chapter 7: Be Present*). Or listen to a guided meditation like I did. You can find numerous free meditations on YouTube or the free app Insight Timer.

Practice choosing your feelings when there's not much going on, like now. How would you like to feel this moment? *Choose* to feel it. Close your eyes and imagine experiencing that feeling now. Bathe in that energy for as long as you like.

Practice choosing your feelings as often as you can. Don't wait until you feel bad. You can feel great and can choose to feel even better. There's no limit to how amazing you can feel.

MINIMALIST MANTRAS

- I can choose how I want to feel.
- There's always space to feel even better.
- There's no limit to how wonderful I can feel and how good my life can get.

Chapter 17
Curiosity

A great tool to let go of old, stale thinking that no longer supports you is curiosity. It's powerful and helps you end negative thoughts quickly!

The next time you're caught up in unhelpful thoughts that bring you down, shift into curiosity. How do you do that? By asking one or several of the following questions.

- Could something else be true, too?
- Is there another way to look at this?
- Could I change my mind about this?
- How could this turn into the best thing that's ever happened to me?
- What if I looked at it from the opposite perspective? Perhaps what I think is bad for me is actually *good* for me?
- What if none of my thoughts were true?
- Because I can choose my own truth, what do I choose to believe?
- Because I can choose how I want to feel, what do I choose to feel?
- How else could I interpret this situation?
- What positive meaning could I give to this experience?
- I'm curious to see how this will work out in my favor!

Curiosity opens and clears your mind. It helps you release outdated beliefs and shift your ability to look at life in new and exciting ways. It expands your opportunities and the possibilities you can see. It enhances your creativity. A curious mind is flexible, open, expansive, spacious, and creative. When you explore what else might be possible or true, your mind automatically quiets down. It's impossible to be curious and feel overwhelmed or feel down at the same time. Try it!

MINIMALIST MANTRAS

- The more I treasure my curiosity, the more alive I feel.
- The more curious I am, the more creativity and freedom I experience.
- Curiosity calms my nerves and opens me to bigger and better possibilities and experiences.

———————

You can sign up for bonus gifts at www.innerminimalistgifts.com and receive a beautiful PDF with these questions that help you clear your mind and shift your mindset to be more curious. Print them or save them on your computer so you have them near you when you need them.

CHAPTER 18
LOVE YOUR MIND

Love your mind. Appreciate everything it does for you. It can think things through, chew on interesting concepts, and come up with smart ideas. Your brain helps you process information, releases hormones, regulates your blood pressure, and so much more. You have every reason to LOVE it!

Yes, your mind can get cluttered and hinder you from time to time. That's why I share these decluttering tools so your mind can optimally serve you. But there's NO REASON to dislike your mind or look down on it. Yes, you are SO MUCH more than your mind, as you will read in Part Three. Your rational mind is part of your human self, and you're so much more (and so much more powerful) than that. Though it's only a small part of you, it doesn't mean your rational mind isn't something to enjoy and appreciate! The more you love it, the more it can lovingly support you. The universe doesn't make mistakes and the human body, including your mind, is a beautiful, perfect creation. Your soul can experience and enjoy this earthly life thanks to your body and mind. Don't belittle it or want it to be different than it is. Learn to make the most of what you have instead. The tools in this book are here to help you with this, to quiet your mind so you're happier and your mind is free to serve you. That will massively improve your life!

MINIMALIST MANTRAS

- I love my mind and all the great things it does for me.
- My intuition and soul always guide me. My rational mind helps me better implement their guidance.

Chapter 19
Brain Detox

Be mindful of what you feed your brain. When you put garbage in, garbage will come out. When you put love in, love will come out. The less crap you feed your brain, the less crap you need to clear out.

I'm not talking about actual food—although some foods, like walnuts, are said to be good for your brain. Eating healthy and taking good care of yourself benefit your overall health and well-being, including your brain.

I'm talking about other things you feed your brain: the movies you watch, the books you read, the conversations you have, the people you allow into your life. Pay conscious attention to ALL of the information and input you allow into your awareness. How does what you read, see, talk about, listen to, and surround yourself with make you feel? Does it uplift you? Is it constructive? Does it bring you amusement, joy, happiness? Does it make you feel good? Or does it drag you down? Make you feel worse? Does it trigger worries and fears? Does it make you feel overwhelmed or stressed?

I stopped watching mainstream news many years ago. Before that, I watched the news and read the paper almost daily. I thought it was important to stay informed on what was going on in the world. But it only made me feel bad. The mainstream media are incredibly fear focused. They only show a teeny tiny portion of what goes on in the world. Their news didn't support me. These days, I scan the headlines now and then. That's all I need.

For me, it's better to limit my intake of news, but that may not be true for you. If you enjoy mainstream news and it brings you something you want or need, continue to consume it. We're different and I don't know what kind of input serves you. It's up to YOU to be aware of that and feed your mind quality content and input, whatever that looks like for you.

Just remember, the less crap you put in, the less crap you have to clear out.

MINIMALIST MANTRAS

- I pay attention to what I feed my brain, and I make sure it's constructive and uplifting.
- The better the input I allow into my awareness, the better the quality of my life is.

PART THREE

THE TRUTH ABOUT YOU

INTRODUCTION TO PART THREE

You are alive and having a human experience. But there's so much more to you, as this part of the book will show you!

If you experience life from your human self *alone*, you miss out on an ocean of inner calm, peace, quiet, wisdom, and trust that's always available to you. Living from your human perspective often equals living inside your head *only*. This contributes to feeling small, busy, empty, unfulfilled, and unhappy. There's only so much your human self can do and experience. When you learn to tap into ALL that you are and live from that much bigger perspective, many doors open up for you. You gain access to more calm, wisdom, opportunities, and power.

Knowing who and what you TRULY are brings a lot of rest, peace, meaning, fulfillment, and happiness. Tapping into the vastness of your true self wipes out the clutter in your mind. Busyness, overwhelm, overthinking, and stress all disappear the moment you tune into all that you are.

This part of the book shows you who you really are, and how different your experience of life becomes when you live it from another perspective.

It's only when you live from the perspective of your small, human self that your mind is busy and filled with negative, destructive thoughts and destructive self-talk.

When you live from the higher perspective of who you REALLY are, your internal wars and conflicts disappear, and quiet and happiness take their place.

Part Thee of the book shows you the truth of you are. Part Four shows you how to live in alignment with this truth.

Enjoy!

CHAPTER 1
WHO YOU REALLY ARE

You're so much more than your human self. You're a spark of the divine. You're a magnificent being of light expressing itself in human form.

The key is to realize that *you're a soul having a human experience.* People often think that human beings have souls, but that's not the case. You are pure consciousness. When your body dies, your soul lives on. It's just your human form that ceases to exist.

You're an individuated part of All-That-Is, of life itself, of the universe, The Field, God, Goddess, or whatever you like to call it. The key in this sentence is that *you're part of it.* It's impossible to be disconnected from life, from the universe or from your soul. *It's who you ARE.* You cannot exist outside All-That-Is for you are a part of All-That-Is.

Your soul chose to express itself and have a human experience in the body you live in. You chose your personality and your family. This may be hard to grasp. Maybe you can understand this concept intellectually but not really understand what it means. Maybe you believe it without understanding any of it. I hear you. I completely believe all the above. I *know* it without knowing how I know. It just resonates with my deepest truth.

For me, believing this is ALSO a choice. I have no proof. Sure, many spiritual traditions talk about how you're a soul having a human experience and have been talking about it for thousands of years. But rational, actual, factual *proof?* I don't know of any. BUT to my knowledge, there's also NO proof that any of this is UNtrue.

This means you can *choose* what you believe. Do you choose to believe that all you are is your small human self? Do you choose to believe that you're a soul having a human experience? Or do you choose to believe something else? IT'S YOUR CHOICE. So choose to believe something that makes you feel good. That's what I did. Believing I'm a soul having a human experience brings me joy, peace, and gives meaning to my life. It makes me happy and even though I don't *really* understand the details of it all, believing this helps simplify my life and helps me enjoy it much more.

If you want to live a happier, simpler, quieter, richer, fuller, more joyful, and more peaceful life—and you do, or else you wouldn't be reading this book—choose beliefs that support that kind of life.

If you want to believe that life is meaningless and has no purpose, I won't try to convince you of something else. The only thing I'll do is ask you to examine that belief: Does it make you feel good? Does it ring true in the deepest depths of your being? Does it help you live the life you long for? Does it bring you joy? Does it make you feel happy and at peace?

If so, hang on to these beliefs. But if not, I invite you to use the tools I gave in the previous chapters to clear that mind-clutter. I invite you to open up to what I believe to be the truth of you: You're a magnificent being of light expressing itself in human form. A spark of the divine. An individuated part of All-That-Is. A soul having a human experience.

When you live your life from this perspective (while being grounded in your body and your human self!), EVERYTHING changes. Your life becomes so much richer, happier, and abundant on all levels and in all ways. Will you never worry or feel unhappy again? Of course you will! This human experience and all the emotions that go with it are part of your life, too! Your soul *chose* this human experience, remember? If your soul wanted to live as a blue blob on the planet Econ 5, you'd be a blue blob living on Econ

5. That's not what your soul chose, though. She chose to be YOU in THIS body living THIS life, so she could experience everything a human life offers.

So what's the benefit of living from the perspective of your soul? Your life will be lighter and more beautiful. You'll feel calmer and enjoy your life more. When you feel like shit or something lousy happens, you'll be able to move through it quicker and with more ease. You won't get tied up in needless drama anymore. You'll know how to handle it. Your issues or sadness won't take over. YOU are at the wheel of your life and you're steering it with faith, strength, and joy.

The next chapters share more about your small human self versus your Big Self and the vastness of all that you are. The goal of this section is to help you integrate this knowledge in your life and, more importantly, to help you to live your life from your soul's perspective.

MINIMALIST MANTRAS

- I'm a magnificent being of light expressing itself in human form.
- I'm a spark of the divine.
- I'm a soul having a human experience.

Chapter 2

Your Small Self Versus Your Big Self

The previous chapter described the true nature of you, which I call your Big Self. Your small self is your human self. Your Big Self encompasses your small self. When you live from the perspective of your Big Self, you still live the human experience. You don't suddenly float three feet above the ground, defying gravity, living on light because you no longer need food. *Could* that be possible? I don't see why not. At the moment, however, that's not what my life looks like, and I guess that yours doesn't either.

Living from the perspective of your Big Self doesn't take away your human experience; it adds extra layers of beauty, serenity, calm, strength, abundance, love, and joy. It helps you worry and stress less. You're no longer trapped in a limited version of life and yourself. From this viewpoint, you see more possibilities and options, and you can let go of most of the stuff your mind is preoccupied with. Living from this higher perspective is THE best way to feel relaxed and free. You rise above your stories and beliefs. You can see that you are not your thoughts—you're the one experiencing them. You can see that you're not your experiences—you're the one observing them. You can see that you're not the different roles you play, you're not your personality, you're not defined by your success, where you live, what you look like or what you do.

You're the one who encompasses, contains, and observes it all. Everything exists, but it's not you. There's so much more to you than what you feel, think, or experience. SO much more.

It's like the small toe on your left foot. Or better yet, its toenail. It's there, but it's not ALL that you are. It's part of you, but it doesn't define you. Your left little toenail has an experience of its own now, and if you focus on it you might feel it, but it's just a *small part* of your experience. There's so much more going on and playing out at the same time. Your small self is like that toenail. Your Big Self is like your body. This is a simplified image, but hopefully gives you a better understanding of your small self versus your Big Self.

You can tell from which perspective you experience life by how you feel and what you think. That shows you whether your small of Big Self is currently in charge. You can then consciously choose to shift your perspective. Here's how you can identify which self is in charge.

SMALL SELF

In short: when you experience ANY kind of limitation or negative thought or feeling, you're coming at life from your small self. This means that every time you experience any of the below, your human self is in charge.

- anger
- fear
- overwhelm
- worry
- stress
- feeling a lack of anything (time, money, love, joy, happiness, trust, faith, etc.)
- feeling rushed
- wanting to be in control
- trying to figure something out on your own

- wondering HOW you can achieve something or get something done
- doubts, etc.

In general: every time you don't feel good, you're looking through the lens of your limited human self.

BIG SELF

In short: when you experience feelings of well-being, you experience life from a higher perspective: the perspective of your soul. When you experience any of the below, your Big Self is present.

- love
- trust / faith
- inner calm, inner peace
- joy
- abundance
- a feeling of completeness or wholeness
- knowing the powers of the universe are at your beck and call
- feeling that you're not alone and everything you manifest and achieve is a co-creation between you and the universe, etc.

In general: when you feel trust, faith, joy, love and other feelings that lift your spirits, you're looking at life through the lens of your soul.

When you notice how you feel and realize you don't feel good, that's how you know it's time to shift yourself out of the perspective of your small self. One way to do this is to use the steps and tools I gave you in Part Two, which help you clear the clutter of your mind. Another way is to consciously shift into the perspective of your Big Self. I provide several ways to do that in Part Four, and in Part Five, I show you how I do that myself. For now, all you need to do is let the truth of who you are sink in.

All you need to live a happy, meaningful, free, and fulfilling life is to live life in full alignment with your soul. All you need to experience feelings of peace, calm and anything else you desire is to live life in full alignment with your soul. That's *truly* all you need. It's just not that simple to implement, because the ONLY thing we were taught to work with is our rational mind and our human self. That's why I added Parts One and Two to this book. Often these tools are easier to implement than the tools I share in Parts Four and Five.

By giving you exercises and ways to operate on both your human and soul level, you can choose which tools work best for you. This can vary day by day, by the way. Something that works wonders for you today may not work at all tomorrow. Just pick whatever tool speaks to you the moment you need it.

Before we dive into how you can shift into your soul's perspective, there's one more thing to go over first. You need to know which common thoughts are ALL lies, and which thoughts are actually the truth.

MINIMALIST MANTRAS

- Living from the perspective of my soul adds extra value and layers of love, abundance, and joy to my human experience.
- All I have to do to lead a happy, fulfilling life is to live in alignment with my soul.

CHAPTER 3
THESE ARE ALL LIES

When you realize you're a divine being of light, this means that you are whole. You're already complete. You're part of the universe and connected to everything and everyone else. And you have access to the limitless powers and wisdom of the universe.

Any thought that contradicts ANYTHING above is untrue. It can *feel* true. But it really isn't. Here are some examples of common thoughts that feel true but are, in fact, lies.

Lie: Any thought that tells you that you are powerless, small, or weak.

Truth: Pure consciousness knows no limits or weaknesses. You *are* pure consciousness expressing itself in human form. Your human self may feel frail or fragile, and you can think that you're vulnerable or paralyzed, but that's not who you are and it's not your true nature.

Lie: Any thought that tells you there's something wrong with you.

Truth: The universe, All-That-Is, The Field, Life, Tao, Goddess, God or whatever you choose to call it, doesn't make mistakes. Everything is as it should be, always. Including you. Your mind or other people can tell you there's something wrong with you, but that's not the case. There isn't. And there never was.

Lie: Any thought that tells you that you're alone and have to do everything yourself.

Truth: Your human self can be without friends and family, yes. And you can certainly *feel* abandoned and alone. But from the perspective of your Big Self, you're never alone. You're a part of the divine, a part of life, connected to All-That-Is. An individuated part of it, yes, but still a part of it. You're never alone, disconnected from life, or separate from All-That-Is. It's impossible. Not much is impossible, but this is.

There are endless thoughts that are lies so I can't list them all, even if I wanted to. I'll give you a beautiful, powerful journal question to help you uncover your own lies and truths instead.

JOURNAL PROMPT

Next time you feel bad about yourself, explore which thought(s) make you feel that way. Play with this prompt by asking yourself the questions below and see what you come up with. Notice how different you feel.

> Is this belief in line with my true nature?
> If not, what is?

If this prompt doesn't work for you or confuses you, skip it. There are plenty of other tools in this book to play with. Use one of them to clear your mind and feel better.

MINIMALIST MANTRAS

- I am already whole.
- I am already complete.
- There is nothing wrong with me and there never was.

PART FOUR

HOW TO LIVE FROM YOUR SOUL

INTRODUCTION TO PART FOUR

It's one thing to realize that your human self is only a small part of what and who you truly are: an individual spark of the divine, pure consciousness expressing itself in human form. It's another thing to live in alignment with this knowledge. How *do* you live your life from the perspective of your soul? What does that look like?

That's what the following chapters show you. Use and play with one or more concepts that speak to you. Everything I share with you works. But you're the only one who knows what works for *you*.

Go through the chapters and notice what resonates with you or what shifts something inside you. The idea that jumps out to you is the practice you'll most benefit from.

Practice living from the perspective of your soul as often as you can. Spend time to consciously connect with your inner wisdom regularly—daily if you can! It adds more joy, ease, calm, and peace to your life.

When you consciously bond with your soul and her energy, you transcend your busy mind. The energy of your soul is so much brighter and lighter than the energy of your rational mind. This increased energy melts away all lower, denser energies, like those of fear, worry, overwhelm, or stress.

Your energy shifts and increases as a result of working on your mindset. The tools in Part Two helped you do that. Living from the perspective of your soul makes raising your energy faster and easier. When your energy or vibration is high, worries and cares melt away like ice cream in the sun. After all, everything is energy, including your fears and doubts. You don't even have to know what causes them in order to shift them. That's what increasing your energy, or raising your vibration, does for you. Your energy automatically increases when you consciously cultivate your connection with soul, spirit, the universe, and life itself, and the following chapters help you learn how to do this.

CHAPTER 1
WHAT WOULD MY SOUL DO?

The quickest way to shift into and live from the perspective of your soul is to ask one of these questions and act on the answers that come up.

- What would my soul do?
- How would she act?
- What would she say?
- What would she think?
- How would she respond?
- How would she feel?

Answer these questions throughout the day. Ask them *especially* when you feel down, scared, annoyed, or triggered by anything or anyone. Act on the answers that come up as much as you can.

The more you practice, the easier it is to live in that higher energy of your soul, your big self. It gradually becomes your default state. This takes regular and conscious practice and awareness. It's THE way to live a calmer, quieter and happier life. It's the way to live in flow and to feel at peace even when shit hits the fan. You'll be able to move through negative feelings or situations sooner and experience more joy than ever.

You can only feel down, overwhelmed, stressed, hopeless or scared when you come from your human self. Your soul knows none of these feelings. If you want to experience *true* calm, peace, love, and joy, your soul is where it's at!

Practice asking the questions above as often as you can. Pay attention to your thoughts, actions, and words. The more you align everything you do with all that you truly are, the more you align with your soul, the more powerful, happy, and at peace you will feel.

This morning I felt anxious about a situation. Instead of jumping on a train of negative thoughts, I asked myself what my soul would do. How would my soul respond? The answer came quickly: the best thing to do was to trust that this situation would work out somehow. It wasn't necessary to give these circumstances any more of my attention. I should focus on something else now. This advice calmed me down and felt true, so I followed it.

A couple of hours later I suddenly had a brainwave to take an action that solved the issue. I'm certain this idea could only come to me because I calmed down and stopped thinking about my problem. This opened the door for the solution to come to me. I'm glad I asked my soul for advice and listened to it. In my experience, my soul always knows what's best!

MINIMALIST MANTRAS

- The more I let my soul guide my life, the more flow and happiness I experience.
- My soul knows no fear, no doubts, no overwhelm and no stress.

Chapter 2

Surrender and Let Your Soul Take the Lead

Surrender means to let go of your worries, fears, dreams, and desires. Surrender is to stop micromanaging the shit out of every detail, out of *life*, and to start *living* instead. Surrender means to choose to trust in something greater than yourself and to choose to have faith in life.

Surrender is a concept most people struggle with. Every time I point out to a client that it's time to let go of their resistance, desire, or struggle, I always get the same reaction. They agree it's time to let go yet don't want to do that at the same time. They wonder if it's really safe to surrender and *how* you can do it.

I understand. I find it hard to surrender sometimes, too. I used to fear it might open the door to more negativity. I feared that when I let go, nothing would get done and no one would pick up the slack. I'm *much* better at letting go than a few years ago, but these thoughts still cross my mind at times.

I remember *really* struggling with something once. I *knew* the solution was to surrender, but I just wouldn't let go. So I asked my spirit guides to help me. They gave me a beautiful message that helps me to this day. I share it here in the hopes it helps you as well.

"All you have to surrender to is each moment. Each now. And to what your soul guides you to do in each moment. Remember:

you don't surrender to something or someone outside of you. You surrender to the biggest, most expansive version of yourself since you *are* life, you *are* part of All-That-Is. You hand things over to your Highest Self. To the part of you that *knows*. To your True Self who dreamt up this human form.

Your human form is part of who you are, too! There's just a bigger part of you that contains it all: your human form and experiences, including all your thoughts, feelings and emotions. Your divine self is part of you as well. It is all you. And you can choose to live from your human or your divine perspective. To surrender means to consciously choose to let your divine self guide you and take the lead.

You are free to choose. Know that the divine perspective is all there is in the end. *That's* where all your power is. *That's* where unlimited options are. *That's* where pure joy and love are."

The key insight from this message—for me—is that you don't surrender to anything or anyone outside of yourself. You surrender to the biggest, most expansive version of yourself.

Surrender your hopes, dreams, fears, and needs. Hand them over to your soul. Let her handle the details and bring you what you need. All you have to do is follow her lead. You do that by following your passion and your joy, your excitement, your intuition, your inner wisdom, and your deep down *knowing*.

That's how you surrender to your soul and life itself. That's how you let your soul guide your life. And *that's* how you act on the wisdom of your soul instead of following the often fear-based guidance of your rational mind.

MINIMALIST MANTRAS

- I let my soul handle the details of my life.
- My soul guides me.
- I surrender to my soul, the highest, wisest part of who I AM.

Chapter 3

Questions That Shift Your Perspective

Your human self asks different questions than your soul self does. Asking different questions leads to different answers. Asking higher-level questions gives you higher-level answers and a better perspective. Questions that reflect your limited human perspective are questions like these.

- Why does this always happen to me?
- What's wrong with me?
- What am I doing wrong?
- Why can't I change this?
- Why do I keep … ? fill in the blank with what you keep doing or experiencing
- Why is everyone against me?
- Why can't I … ? fill in the blank with what you think is impossible for you

What these questions have in common is that they feel restrictive. They ooze an energy of hopelessness, powerlessness, and despair. They reflect the limitations of your rational mind and will generate answers that reflect the same limitations.

An easy way to shift into the perspective of your soul is to ask different questions. Questions that open the door to opportunity instead of limitation, that uplift you instead of bring you down, that help you see a different perspective instead of rehash the same old thoughts you're always thinking. Asking these questions helps you access the higher perspective of your soul.

- What message does this situation have for me?
- How does this situation help me heal?
- How does this situation help me grow?
- What's the gift of this experience?
- What does this experience open me up to?
- How does this experience allow me to let more love and joy into my life?
- How does this help me grow?
- How is this situation / experience the answer to my prayers?
- What does this situation or experience invite me to do?
- What can I let go of thanks to this experience?

Do you notice how different these questions make you feel? Can you sense how they soothe you, soften your feelings, and open you up? Do you feel more spacious, lighter, and uplifted? I definitely feel that myself, just from reading these questions.

Reminder: do not use these questions to bypass or suppress your emotions or pain!!! If you feel resistance when you try to answer these questions, or they make you feel mad and sad, STOP. There are emotions you still need to let out or process. DO THAT FIRST. Only come back to these questions when you feel ready to answer them.

I recently used one of these questions after I hurt my back during a workout. I asked myself what the gift of this experience was. The answer was clear: this pain taught me to better listen to my body and the signals it gives me. The pain was also a reminder to pay more attention to my form and not rush through the workouts. Lesson learned. ;-) (And yes, I also went to a physical therapist to help me heal.)

MINIMALIST MANTRA

- The better the questions I ask, the better the answers I receive.

———————

You can sign up for bonus gifts at www.innerminimalistgifts. com and receive a beautiful PDF with these questions that help you shift into the perspective of your soul. Print them or save them on your computer so you have them near you when you need them.

Chapter 4

The One Question That Changes Everything

This question is a variation on the journal prompt I gave you in Part Three, Chapter 3. But it's so powerful and beautiful that I wanted to share it with you in a separate chapter as well to make sure you don't miss it. Use it every time you think a thought that brings you down, even if only a little.

Journal Prompt

Does this belief represent the limitlessness and abundance of your soul? If not, what does?

Here are some examples of how you can work with this question.

Thought: I'm not good enough.
Does this belief represent the limitlessness and abundance of your soul? No.
What does? I'm good enough, exactly as I am. I'm good enough for what I need to do.

Thought: It's impossible for me to achieve my dreams.
Does this belief represent the limitlessness and abundance of your soul? No.

What does? I'm more powerful than I think. I have access to limitless options and opportunities. My dreams and deep desires come straight from my soul. I'm meant to experience and manifest them, and my soul is by my side to help me realize them!

Thought: I'm too scared to move forward.
Does this belief represent the limitless and abundance of your soul? No.
What does? I can do anything I set my mind to. I'm much bigger than my fears.

Play with this question and see what opens up for you.

MINIMALIST MANTRA

* I'm an unlimited being with unlimited power, love, and opportunities.

Chapter 5
You're Always Connected

People often think they can lose the connection with their soul and need to *do* something to restore it. That's never necessary. There's nothing you have to do to reconnect with your soul because you were never disconnected from it to begin with. All you have to do is *stop* doing whatever made you feel disconnected, and the problem is usually believing thoughts that tell you you're disconnected. This book offers you tools to help you shift those thoughts. Just remind yourself it's impossible to lose the connection with your soul because you ARE soul. The moment you remember this, you can find your inner peace again. That place of inner peace is always available to you because it IS you. It's never not there. You find it underneath your thoughts, your busyness, your worries and your stress. You find it when you remember that you're always connected to your soul. You're always connected to life and the universe because you're a part of it.

Knowing that you're never disconnected can help you feel more safe and secure in the world, in your life, and in your skin. Remember that you're never disconnected from your soul. That's impossible because YOU. ARE. SOUL.

For a while I had a background on my phone that said, "I AM SOUL." I saw this reminder every time I picked up my phone. I kept it on my phone until I no longer needed that reminder.

Today, my background says, "ALL I have to do is align with Source, Self and what I want. It REALLY is THAT simple!" It reminds me that manifesting my dreams is about being aligned with my soul and following her guidance in each moment. It reminds me that I don't have to know how I can accomplish my big dreams, because my soul does. As soon as I no longer need this reminder, I'll create a new one.

MINIMALIST MANTRAS

- It's impossible to be disconnected from my soul because I AM soul.
- It's impossible to be disconnected from the universe, because I AM a part of the universe, a part of the whole.

Chapter 6
Relax

You feel relaxed and at peace when you operate from the perspective of your soul. It works the other way around, too: you automatically shift into the perspective of your soul when you relax, and it's easier to access all of your power, intuition and wisdom.

When you relax, your mind quiets down. It's impossible to feel relaxed and have an overactive mind at the same time.

So relax. You can do that right now, while you read. Relax your forehead and eyebrows. Soften your eyes. Relax your jaw, your mouth, and your tongue. Drop your shoulders. Gently and slowly, roll your head. Start breathing deeper and slower. Shift in your seat so your body feels more comfortable.

Do you feel the difference? You're still reading. You're still sitting in the same room. Everything is the same. Yet you're more relaxed than you were before.

This is how you can relax while you work, while you read, while you do *anything*. When you relax your body, your mind follows. There's no other way. You can't breathe deeply and panic at the same time. When you're stressed or scared, your breaths are shallower and faster. This makes you freak out even more. The moment you slow everything down, you calm down. To help you learn to breathe deeper, put your hand on your belly and focus on feeling your belly rise and drop as you inhale and exhale. Focus on that until you feel calmer.

When you relax, your rational mind is calm enough to serve you instead of distract you. When you relax, negative thoughts can no longer bring you down.

MINIMALIST MANTRAS

- When I relax my body, my mind follows.
- The more I relax, the calmer and happier I feel.

CHAPTER 7

BE PRESENT

Are you *fully* present in each moment? If you're like most people, you're not. That's because most of the time your thoughts focus on the past or the future. You endlessly think about what has already been or what's not here yet.

But you can't act in the past or in the future. You can't access your full power in the past or in the future. You can't access your creativity or intuition in the past or the future. You can ONLY act now. Your full power, creativity and intuition are ONLY available to you in this moment.

When your thoughts revolve around the past or the future, you miss what this moment has to offer. Life passes you by when your focus is everywhere but right here, right now. You miss beauty and joy. You worry about things that aren't here yet and may never happen! You worry about things you can't change because they already happened. Worrying is pointless and only leads to more suffering, worry, and struggling.

If you want to have a clear and focused mind, and if you want to have full access to your power and creativity and live life to the fullest, you need to be present.

One way to get present is to bring your full attention to what you're seeing, hearing, feeling, tasting, and sensing in this moment. Let's focus on your hearing first. Close your eyes. This helps you turn inward, be more present, and avoid distractions. What sounds do you hear, nearby and far away? Pay attention to what you see (yes, with your eyes closed). Next, focus on what you can smell, followed by what you can taste. Finally, notice how your body feels. Do this exercise several times per day.

When you practice being present, you'll soon notice how much calmer you feel. You feel more relaxed. You worry less. Your stress reduces. You feel more energy and have a clearer mind. It's easier to focus and to come up with ideas and solutions. Being present has many benefits and you experience them quickly!

Your breath is also a beautiful tool to help you get present. Deepen your inhalations and exhalations, feeling how every breath relaxes you a little more.

You can enhance your present moment awareness by being mindful about what you do in each moment. Consciously taste and enjoy each bite of your sandwich. Wash your hair with care instead of on autopilot. Give your full attention to whatever you do and you'll become present with yourself, your body, this moment, and your life.

The more you focus on this moment, the better you feel and the more creative, powerful, and intuitive you are. The more present you are, the calmer your mind is. Worries and fears melt away. You can feel that in this moment, all is well. In this moment, you are okay. And in this moment. And in this one.

In this moment, all is always well.

MINIMALIST MANTRAS

- This moment is everything.
- Everything I need and want is available to me in this moment.
- In this moment, all is always well.

CHAPTER 8
MEDITATE

Meditation is a wonderful way to become more present and feel less rushed. Research has proven that meditation lowers stress levels and has multiple health benefits. Meditation enhances your immune system, too, for example. Google it if you want to know more, but for now, just accept that meditation is exceptionally good for you. :-)

What's important to remember, though, is that meditation is NOT about *not thinking*. Thoughts are always present. The moment you sit down to meditate and quiet your mind is the moment you notice HOW BUSY IT IS IN THERE. Buddhists call this the monkey mind—it means your mind is restless. Thoughts jump around like monkeys swing from tree branch to tree branch.

Meditation is not about *not* thinking, but about *not getting sucked into* your thoughts. Meditation is about letting your thoughts be and observing them *without* following them. Meditation quiets the mind. Now, you probably won't experience the quiet every time. If you do, great! But don't despair when your mind stays busy. The simple act of choosing to meditate is beneficial in that it calms your mind even when you think it didn't work.

I remember meditating for fifteen minutes once and feeling annoyed that my thoughts kept bouncing all over the place. I did NOT experience much quiet or inner calm! But when my partner saw me walk into the living room after this "failed" meditation session, he said, "Wow! I can see how much this quiet time did for you. You look less stressed and more energized." Ha! That helped me realize that I *did* feel calmer after I meditated, even though my mind had been busy. Meditating still worked for me. And after this experience I stopped judging my meditation time. I simply meditate without expectations or opinions on how I experienced it.

You can meditate in many ways. You can count your breaths, repeat a mantra, stare into a flame, or listen to a guided meditation. You can also do a moving meditation if that speaks to you more. Put on some music, close your eyes, and start moving. Let your body make any maneuver it wants to make, whether it's dancing, jumping, rolling your shoulders, or anything else. If you feel like making sounds, do that, too. Moving your body is easy and doesn't take more than a couple of minutes. Once you start to feel relaxed you can stop. Stretch a bit, lean forward and backward, and notice how your body feels.

MINIMALIST MANTRAS

- Meditation makes me feel better, even if my mind jumps all over the place.
- Everything can be a meditation when I give it my full attention, do it with care, and I'm fully present in the moment.

CHAPTER 9
INTUITION

Your soul guides you every second of every day. She does that via hunches, coincidences, symbols, dreams, synchronicities, and above all, your intuition. If you want to live from your soul and find more peace and calm in your life, you need to follow your intuition. Following your intuition enhances your well-being, helps you make better decisions, and manifest with less effort.

The more frequently you follow your intuition, the more you learn to trust it, the more you benefit from it, and the calmer your mind becomes. You free up your mind to support you to act efficiently and intelligently on your intuition. Your intuition rules, your mind is its servant.

You don't have to wait for your intuition to bring you information. You can practice to consciously work with it. But you need to make time to turn inward and notice what your intuition is telling you. Here's a good way to do that.

First make sure you won't be disturbed and close your eyes. Relax your body. Drop your shoulders. Relax your forehead, your eyebrows, and your eyes. Relax your mouth, your jaws and your tongue. Start breathing in and out, deeper and slower.

As soon as you feel more present and relaxed you can open your eyes. Then, write down a question (see examples in the list below). After writing your question, write down *everything* that comes up next. Don't judge or censor anything. The answers don't have to make sense, and you don't have to believe the information comes from your soul. It doesn't matter if your imagination is speaking to you or if you're making it all up, so don't worry about that. *Your soul speaks to you through your imagination as well*. Plus, if the information that comes through inspires you, makes you feel better, and gives you guidance you can follow, who cares if your soul spoke to you, or an angel, an alien, or your imagination? If the information rings true, is loving and kind, and it serves you, that's great!

You can ask as many questions as you like or have time for. Read through your answers when you're ready. Did you receive (new) insights and ideas? How can you act on the information you wrote down?

Practice doing this daily. Once you become more experienced in talking with your soul, you can do it anytime, anywhere, and you no longer need a notebook. You can have a conversation in your mind. But when you're new at this, it helps to write everything down. Writing helps you focus and ensures you don't miss any information.

I used to write down questions for my soul in my journal every day. Sometimes I received new insights or ideas. Sometimes the answers blew my mind. Other times I felt that I was just fantasizing and imagining things.

I kept practicing and acted on the information that felt useful and true. That's how I learned to trust my intuition and my inner wisdom. I learned to recognize how my soul and intuition spoke with me, and I learned to tune into my intuition without writing questions and answers. Now, I no longer need to close my eyes or relax before I can talk with my soul. I'm in a state of constant awareness of the guidance my intuition and soul bring me. And most of the time, I act on it, too.

If you ask a question about something you fear or something that's very important to you, it can be difficult to know if it's your intuition or your fear who answers your question. Start with questions like these.

- What message do you have for me now?
- What's in my highest good to focus on today?
- Is there something that would support my well-being now?
- Is there something I can do now that supports the unfolding of my dreams?
- How can I experience more joy?
- How can I open up to more love?
- What would help me live life more fully?

Write down all answers. Start to act on the answers as much as you can.

Finally, make notes of your intuition practice. Write down when your intuition was right or what happened when you acted on the inspiration you received. This will show you how wise your intuition is and how much you can trust it.

MINIMALIST MANTRAS

- My soul guides me always, every second of every day.
- The more I follow my intuition, the more everything I want and need falls into place.
- My intuition is always right.

CHAPTER 10
OBSERVE

You can easily shift into the perspective of your soul by first stepping into the role of the observer. Observe your thoughts. Observe your feelings. Don't get tangled up in them. *Notice* what you think and how you feel. You are not your thoughts and you are not your feelings. You're the one experiencing and observing them.

When you observe what goes on inside and around you, you begin to look at life from the perspective of your soul. Observing your thoughts and what you feel creates a space that allows you to be curious about what happens next, or to come up with the most constructive response.

When you *respond*, you come from a place of emotional maturity. You act using the wisdom of your highest self with respect for yourself and others.

When you *react*, you lash out. You do the first thing that comes to mind without checking if your actions are the best way to handle this situation.

When you *observe*, your thoughts no longer run you. You're in charge of them, creating a sense of quiet and clarity.

The more you practice observing your thoughts, the easier it becomes to calmly respond in times of upheaval. Your stress or fears won't take over, and if they sometimes do, you can move through them with more ease.

Observing your thoughts is like watching clouds pass by or birds fly over. You see it, but you think nothing about it. You don't attach any emotions or meaning to it. The clouds and the birds are just *there*, and all you do is watch them come and go. Observing your thoughts works exactly the same.

MINIMALIST MANTRAS

- I am not my thoughts, I'm the observer of my thoughts.
- I am not my feelings, I'm the observer of my feelings.

PART FIVE

THE FIVE GUIDELINES

INTRODUCTION TO PART FIVE

I *know* I'm a soul having a human experience, a spark of the divine. I also know that when I live from the perspective of my soul, that's when I feel most happy, light, free, and fulfilled. But I still have to remind myself of who I am, so I don't get sidetracked by my emotions or the state of the world. I still worry and feel overwhelmed, scared, and insecure. Of course I do! All of this is part of the human experience, and there's nothing wrong with that. I allow myself to feel what I feel and to think what I think. But I no longer wallow in my emotions or give away my power to my thoughts. I learned to feel what I need to feel. I learned to shift myself into a higher perspective, into a higher level of energy. To get there sometimes takes working with one of the mindset tools I shared in Part Two. Sometimes it works better to shift into the perspective of my soul. There are several things that help me do that. Everything I shared in Part Four of this book, for starters. Or reading spiritual books or watching spiritual videos.

But sometimes none of this helps. Because I love journaling and writing, I came up with a way that ALWAYS works for me. What I did is write down five guidelines. These guidelines are simple sentences that remind me who I *truly* am and how I believe life *really* works. At first, I simply read through these guidelines each morning. After a while I started incorporating them into my journaling, and I was blown away by how quickly this shifted my energy and mood. My vibration skyrockets every time I work with these guidelines!

In the following chapters I show you exactly how I work with them and how *you* can come up with your *own* guidelines that work specifically for you.

Chapter 1
My Five Guidelines

The idea for these guidelines came to me in the summer of 2020. I'd set the intention to more fully embody my soul. I'd been practicing this for many years, but I desired to live more from my soul's perspective. I felt there was an easier way for me to do this that I was not aware of yet. A way that was an absolutely perfect match for *me*.

Shortly after I set that intention, I felt stressed. I did NOT remember that I'm a soul having a human experience. I also did NOT listen to my own advice to stay with the feeling and explore (and shift) my thoughts. I *knew* this was the best thing to do, but I just didn't feel like it. I decided to distract myself from this lousy feeling and opened Instagram. The first message I saw said:

YOU ARE A BEING OF LIGHT IN HUMAN FORM

My soul and the universe were making sure they got my attention by showing me that message in ALL CAPS. ;-)

It hit me like a bolt of lightning. The moment I read that sentence, my energy shifted *completely*. One moment I felt stressed, restless, worried, and anxious and the next … I felt AMAZING. Completely calm, filled with trust and a deep knowing that everything was fine. I'd *never* experienced such a profound shift from reading just one sentence. *Wow*, I thought, *I should write that sentence down so I can read it every day! This is so helpful!*

But then I got distracted by another Instagram post and five minutes later I was back where I started: feeling restless and stressed. I realized there was no point distracting myself any longer and took out my journal to explore my thoughts and shift them.

As I grabbed my pen I received a text message from a dear friend. It read: "The universe has the best logistics department ever."*

The same damned thing happened: that sentence hit me and instantly snapped me out of my stressed state. NOW I paid attention and stopped distracting myself. I wrote both sentences in my journal, intending to read through them daily.

Over the next couple of weeks, I added three more sentences that had similar effects on me: instant calm. Instant relief. Instant inner peace. This worked a lot quicker than some of the other tools I used!

One day I read through these guidelines, but their magic didn't instantly work, so I decided to write in my journal about each of these statements. As I did—BAM—deep shifts happened again. Now I had two ways to work with my five guidelines: to read through them or journal about them.

At the moment of writing this book, these guidelines still serve me tremendously well. By the time this book is published, I may have picked new ones to work with or not use this tool anymore. It doesn't matter. This works for me now and might work for you, too, so I'm sharing it, anyway.

---

* Turns out this sentence came from my own book *Unmute Your Life - break free from fear & go for what you REALLY want*. A friend texted me how much she loved that sentence. So do I! I just forgot I wrote it myself. :-)

These are my five guidelines and what each of them reminds me of.

Guideline One: I'm a magnificent being of light in human form
This guideline reminds me of who I really am. I'm not a small, powerless human being. I'm a being of light, a soul having a human experience, a spark of the divine. I'm not my thoughts, I'm not my circumstances, I'm not my body, and I'm not any of the roles I play in this life. I'm pure consciousness expressing itself, an individuated part of All-That-Is. Remember, all of this is true for *you*, too!

Guideline Two: The universe has the best logistics department ever
This guideline reminds me of how creation and manifestation truly work. It's a co-creation between my soul, the universe, Life, and myself. It's my job to decide what I want and don't want. It's up to me how I choose to live and feel. If what I want is aligned with my soul, it will come to me. The universe, my soul, Life—everything— works together to bring me what I want and need. They handle the logistics and details. All I have to do is act on my intuition and inspiration. After I take those actions, it's out of my hands and I can let go. All I have to do is feel what my next step is and take it. The universe handles the rest.

Guideline Three: Take charge
I can feel powerless or hopeless sometimes, but that's NOT who I am. See guideline one. I'm more powerful than I think. I have free will. I'm in charge of my thoughts, choices, actions, and decisions. I'm not at the mercy of life, the universe, others, or my circumstances. I can choose how to respond. I can choose what I give my attention to. I can choose how I want to feel. I can choose what I want and how I spend my time. I can choose where to focus all of my energy. I can ask the universe to bring me whatever I want, and it's natural to receive it, NOT because I'm a whiney child who feels entitled to get what she wants when she wants it. But because that's how

the universe works. You always get what you need, which may not always be what you want. What you want is not always in your best interest. Your soul knows. You can trust her.

You can manifest what you want (again, if it's in your best interests to receive it). All you have to do is choose it, feel as if you already have it, and take your inspired actions. That's it. Other than that? There's nothing to do but just BE.

Guideline Four: There's only now

The present moment is EVERYTHING. It's all there ever is. You can only take action now. You can only breathe now. You can only live now. Everything is always and only NOW.

In this moment you have full access to life, love, joy, inspiration, beauty, or anything else you desire. This moment is the ONLY moment you can take action.

In this moment, all is always well. In this moment, you are always okay. This moment is all there is, and it's all you need. This moment is and contains EVERYTHING.

Guideline Five: Fuck it

This guideline reminds me to let go. To surrender. To remember that whatever happens, I'll be fine. My soul, not my small rational mind, knows what's best for me. I can *think* I know, but I don't. My soul can bring me something INFINITELY better than I can come up with in my wildest dreams. My soul can also bring me something "worse." But it's always in my best interests. Things that seem like failures often bring you the biggest gifts!

"Bad" things can always happen, whether or not you let go and surrender. The more you open up and let the universe do its thing (see guideline two), the more everything flows, the easier everything is, and the better you can handle "bad" stuff when it happens.

When you look at life like this, what can go wrong? Plus, one year from now you probably won't remember what you were freaking out over right now. So fuck it, all is well!

These are my five guidelines. I read through them or journal about them. The next chapter shows you how to do that.

Chapter 2

How I Work with the Five Guidelines

Now that you know my guidelines and how I found them, it's time to look at what you can do with them. In this chapter I describe how I use the five guidelines to help shift my thoughts. You can follow my steps or make up your own as you go!

The first thing I do is describe the situation in one or two sentences. It can be a concern, something I worry about, or a decision I need to make. Then I look at that situation from the perspective of each separate guideline. My energy usually starts to shift when I do this using the first two guidelines. I go through the other three for the fun of it, but they are not always necessary.

Here's a real-life example of what this looks like. I copied it directly from my journal.

The situation: I worry about money.

Guideline One: I'm a magnificent being of light in human form
When I look at it from this perspective, there's absolutely nothing to worry about. I'm more powerful than I think. It's my consciousness that creates my outcomes and brings me what I need, including money. It's all energy, after all. I can manifest anything I choose! My options and opportunities are limitless. The universe is abundant and so much more is possible than my small rational mind can

imagine. What my human self can come up with is only a tiny fraction of what my soul is capable of!

Guideline Two: The universe has the best logistics department ever
I don't know where the money can come from, but I don't *have* to know. The universe does! It handles all those details for me. Money can come to me through limitless channels, 24–7. I don't have to know how it can happen or what's possible. The universe brings me the ideas and inspiration I need. It will bring me the money or show me which actions I need to take that will bring money to me. I don't have to figure anything out. That's the universe's job.

Guideline Three: Take charge
I choose to trust that all is well. I decide that money is no issue for me, and it's always there when I need it. All I have to do is follow my inspired actions, and that's it. Show me the money, universe!

I choose to relax. I decide that all the money I spend and invest returns to me at least tenfold. I decide that money always flows to me with ease, regardless of what I'm doing or not doing. I decide I can easily pay for all that I want and need AND still have lots of money to spare. That's the way it is because I decide that this is the way it is!

Guideline Four: There's only now
Oh, right … there's no reason to worry about it at all because in this moment, I'm okay. In this moment, all is well. In this moment, I have no problem. I'm happy, I'm healthy, I have money in the bank and food in the fridge. In this moment, everything is just perfect.

Guideline Five: Fuck it
Why worry about it at all? It serves no purpose and brings me nothing. Everything will work out one way or another. It always has, and it always will. And if for some strange reason it doesn't? It'll still work out somehow.

You may not understand or resonate with what I wrote, but that's because it's from my journal, not yours. :-) Doing this exercise made *me* feel better and released *my* worries. *That's* what matters.

The guidelines that work for you may be different, and the way you journal about your guidelines will be different, too.

It doesn't matter how you journal or if others understand what you wrote. All that matters is that it works for YOU.

In the next chapter, you learn how to pick your personal guidelines, and I give you an example of another way you can work with them.

CHAPTER 3
CREATE YOUR OWN GUIDELINES

If my guidelines resonate with you and you noticed something shift inside you when you read them, use them. If they don't, come up with your own. You don't have to invent them. All you have to do is notice when you read or hear something that instantly lights you up. Notice when you feel a shift, a change, or a space open up that allows you to breathe a little deeper and freer.

You can start by leafing through this book. What chapter(s) spoke to you most? What Minimalist Mantra(s) jumped out for you? What insights did you get? Is there an idea or sentence in this book that shifted something inside you? What resonated with and inspired you?

Write one or more of these sentences and ideas down. Read through them daily. Play around as you write in your journal about them. You can do that right now. You can use an issue that's bothering you and journal about that from the perspective of each separate guideline, like I showed you in the previous chapter.

You can also play with it another way: by asking yourself what would be different if you already deeply believed each guideline and had applied it to your life and business. Here's an example to show you what this can look like.

Let's say your top five insights from this book are the following.

> One: I am not my thoughts.
> Two: I'm a soul having a human experience.
> Three: In this moment, all is well.
> Four: My intuition never steers me wrong.
> Five: My thoughts determine how I feel.

What would be different if you believed each one of these guidelines already and applied them to every aspect of your life? When you journal about that, your answers might look something like this.

Guideline One: I am not my thoughts
If I always remembered that, I'd realize I'm the one observing what I think, and this would create some space between myself and my thoughts. It would make me feel lighter. I'd have power over my thoughts; they wouldn't have any more power over me than I give them. That would make me feel strong and free! I'd know I'm not at the mercy of my thoughts. I'd be able to stop those cycles of negativity and focus on something else. Freedom!

Guideline Two: I'm a soul having a human experience
This reminds me that I'm not just my small human self. There's so much more to me than that! I'm part of the universe and can co-create with my soul and the universe. That's such a relief! I don't have to figure things out and can always ask the universe and my soul for help. I'm not alone and my life has meaning and a purpose. Even when I'm not sure what my purpose is, I trust it *has* a purpose. Believing this would make me feel more powerful and help me have faith in myself.

Guideline Three: In this moment, all is well
If I always remembered that, I'd never worry about anything ever again. I'd feel safe and secure. I'd feel so much calmer. I wouldn't

worry about my to-do list. I'd enjoy each moment more, enjoy my entire *life* more! I'd only have to focus on *this* moment. That feels so much better than constantly mulling over the past or worry about the future!

Guideline Four: My intuition never steers me wrong
If I remembered this, I'd never wonder what to do next or what the best decision would be. It would bring me more peace. If I always trusted my intuition, I'd always know what to do. I'd always know what to focus on and what to ignore. That would save me so much time! It would make my life easier.

Guideline Five: My thoughts determine how I feel
If I could remember that my *thoughts* determine how I feel instead of the situation I'm in, that would open up a new world for me! I wouldn't get carried away by things I have no control over. I'd feel so much more powerful knowing that I can always change how I think and how I feel. It feels amazing to know that I don't need *anyone* or *anything* to change for me to feel better. If I applied this guideline to my daily life, I'd feel happier and freer than ever before! My life would improve immensely.

Use your guidelines in any way that feels right for you. Print them out and hang them where you can look at them daily. Set a reminder on your phone to read through them three times per day. Journal about your guidelines whenever you feel like it.

Feel free to add new guidelines or replace the ones that no longer work for you. Experiment with your inspiring sentences in whatever way feels good to you. Your guidelines are your personal portal to a simpler, quieter, and happier life!

WHAT'S NEXT?

I hope this book inspired you and gave you tools to help you create a calmer mind and a happier life!

If you're looking for more inspiration or support, I've got you covered.

First, you can get complimentary gifts, including an audio file to help you ground and center yourself, a collection of *Minimalist Mantras*, a list of questions that help you shift into the perspective of your soul, and more! Find them here: www.innerminimalistgifts.com

If you'd like to take a deeper dive into what you learned in this book, check out my online program here: www.innerminimalistprogram.com

And come say hi on social media! You can find me here:

Instagram: www.instagram.com/brigitte_van_tuijl/
Facebook: www.facebook.com/brigittevantuijl.artofdivineselfishness/
Twitter: https://twitter.com/brigittevanT

Thank you for reading and playing with this book. I hope you enjoyed it and if so, please leave me a brilliant review! Or just a nice one. That'll make me happy, too. :-)

For now, I wish you all the best, and hope you enjoy a simpler, quieter and happier life!

Love,

Brigitte

OTHER BOOKS BY BRIGITTE

The Gap - bridge the space between where you are and where you want to be
No matter how big your dream or goal is, realizing it can be easier than you think. This book shows you how.

The Art of Divine Selfishness Series

Book One: Unmute Your Life - break free from fear & go for what you REALLY want
This book helps you uncover your TRUE dreams and make them real.

Book Two: The Art of Divine Selfishness - transform your life, your business & the world by putting YOU first
If you want to create a business and life you adore, you need to put yourself first! This book shows you how.

Books in Dutch

Ontdek Wat Je Écht Wilt En Maak Daar (Je) Werk Van
Een praktisch en inspirerend werkboek om zelfstandig in kaart te brengen wat je écht wilt - en daar je werk van te maken.

You can find more information on these books and new books I'm working on at www.booksbybrigitte.com